Walt Disney's Donald Duck

Winks

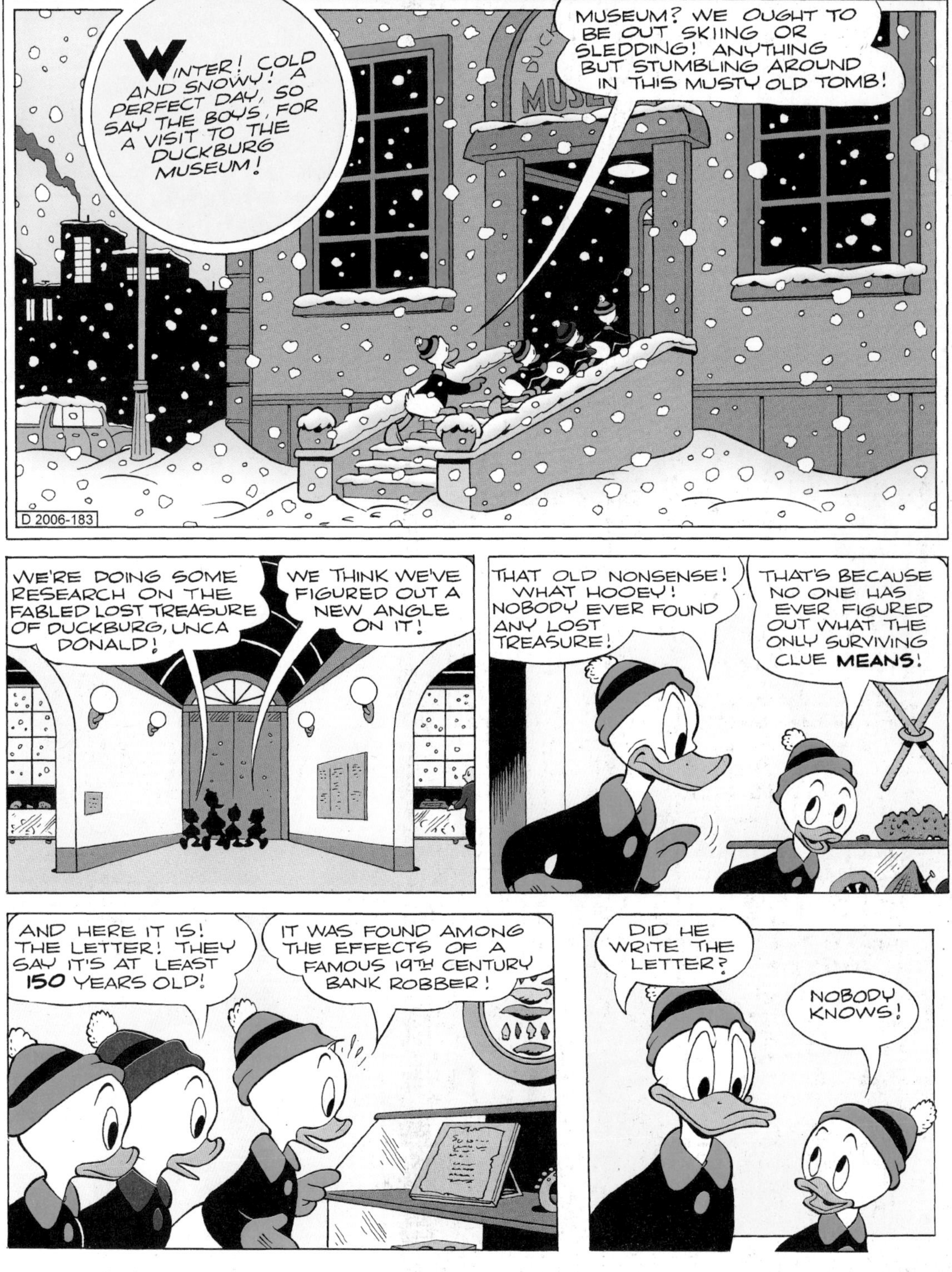
WINTER! COLD AND SNOWY! A PERFECT DAY, SO SAY THE BOYS, FOR A VISIT TO THE DUCKBURG MUSEUM!
MUSEUM? WE OUGHT TO BE OUT SKIING OR SLEDDING! ANYTHING BUT STUMBLING AROUND IN THIS MUSTY OLD TOMB!
D 2006-183
WE'RE DOING SOME RESEARCH ON THE FABLED LOST TREASURE OF DUCKBURG, UNCA DONALD!
WE THINK WE'VE FIGURED OUT A NEW ANGLE ON IT!
THAT OLD NONSENSE! WHAT HOOEY! NOBODY EVER FOUND ANY LOST TREASURE!
THAT'S BECAUSE NO ONE HAS EVER FIGURED OUT WHAT THE ONLY SURVIVING CLUE MEANS!
AND HERE IT IS! THE LETTER! THEY SAY IT'S AT LEAST 150 YEARS OLD!
IT WAS FOUND AMONG THE EFFECTS OF A FAMOUS 19TH CENTURY BANK ROBBER!
DID HE WRITE THE LETTER?
NOBODY KNOWS!

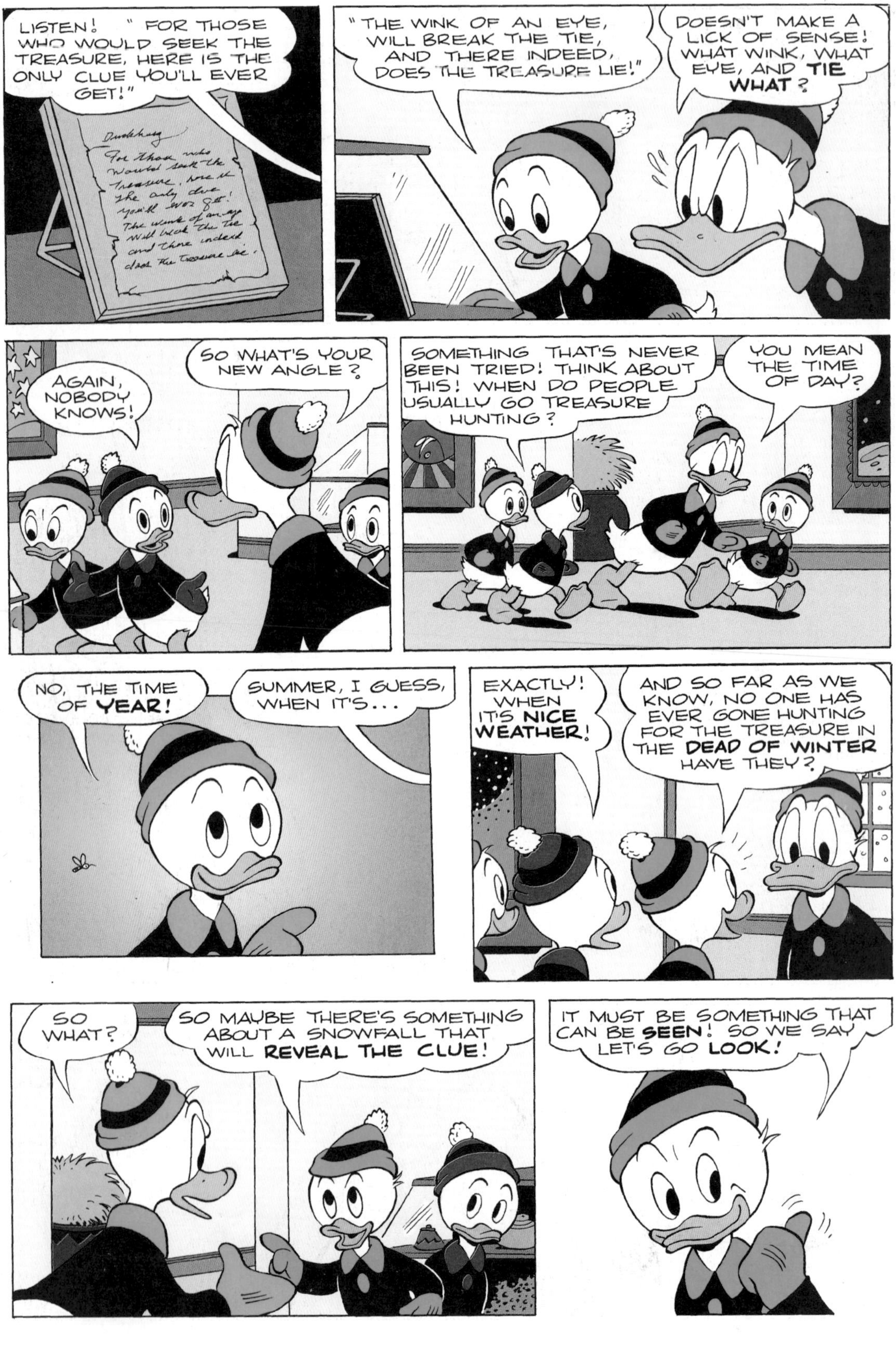

LISTEN! "FOR THOSE WHO WOULD SEEK THE TREASURE, HERE IS THE ONLY CLUE YOU'LL EVER GET!"
"THE WINK OF AN EYE, WILL BREAK THE TIE, AND THERE INDEED, DOES THE TREASURE LIE!"
DOESN'T MAKE A LICK OF SENSE! WHAT WINK, WHAT EYE, AND **TIE WHAT**?
AGAIN, NOBODY KNOWS!
SO WHAT'S YOUR NEW ANGLE?
SOMETHING THAT'S NEVER BEEN TRIED! THINK ABOUT THIS! WHEN DO PEOPLE USUALLY GO TREASURE HUNTING?
YOU MEAN THE TIME OF DAY?
NO, THE TIME OF **YEAR**!
SUMMER, I GUESS, WHEN IT'S...
EXACTLY! WHEN IT'S **NICE WEATHER**!
AND SO FAR AS WE KNOW, NO ONE HAS EVER GONE HUNTING FOR THE TREASURE IN THE **DEAD OF WINTER** HAVE THEY?
SO WHAT?
SO MAYBE THERE'S SOMETHING ABOUT A SNOWFALL THAT WILL **REVEAL THE CLUE**!
IT MUST BE SOMETHING THAT CAN BE **SEEN**! SO WE SAY LET'S GO **LOOK**!

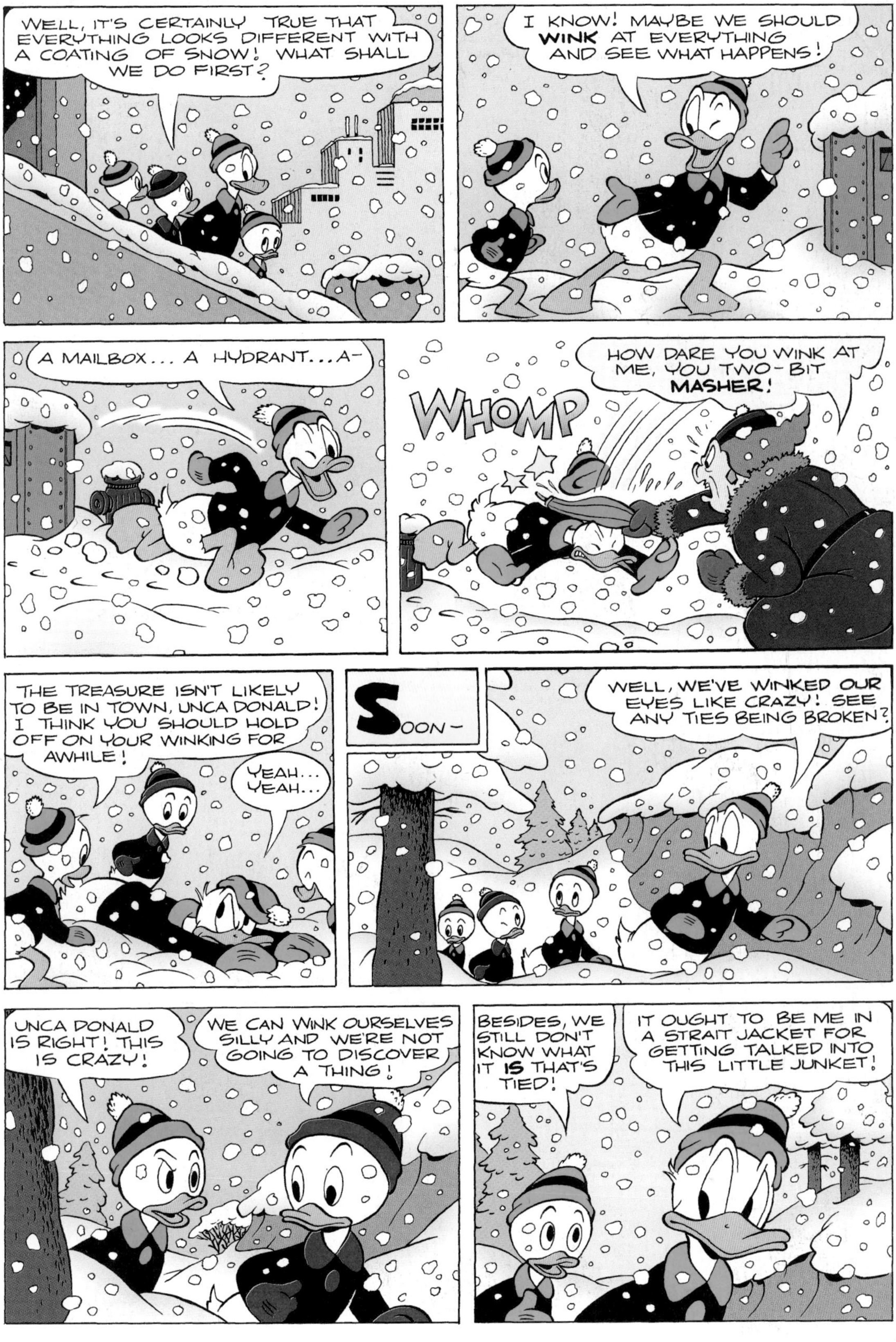
WELL, IT'S CERTAINLY TRUE THAT EVERYTHING LOOKS DIFFERENT WITH A COATING OF SNOW! WHAT SHALL WE DO FIRST?
I KNOW! MAYBE WE SHOULD WINK AT EVERYTHING AND SEE WHAT HAPPENS!
A MAILBOX... A HYDRANT... A-
WHOMP
HOW DARE YOU WINK AT ME, YOU TWO-BIT MASHER!
THE TREASURE ISN'T LIKELY TO BE IN TOWN, UNCA DONALD! I THINK YOU SHOULD HOLD OFF ON YOUR WINKING FOR AWHILE!
YEAH... YEAH...
SOON-
WELL, WE'VE WINKED OUR EYES LIKE CRAZY! SEE ANY TIES BEING BROKEN?
UNCA DONALD IS RIGHT! THIS IS CRAZY!
WE CAN WINK OURSELVES SILLY AND WE'RE NOT GOING TO DISCOVER A THING!
BESIDES, WE STILL DON'T KNOW WHAT IT IS THAT'S TIED!
IT OUGHT TO BE ME IN A STRAIT JACKET FOR GETTING TALKED INTO THIS LITTLE JUNKET!

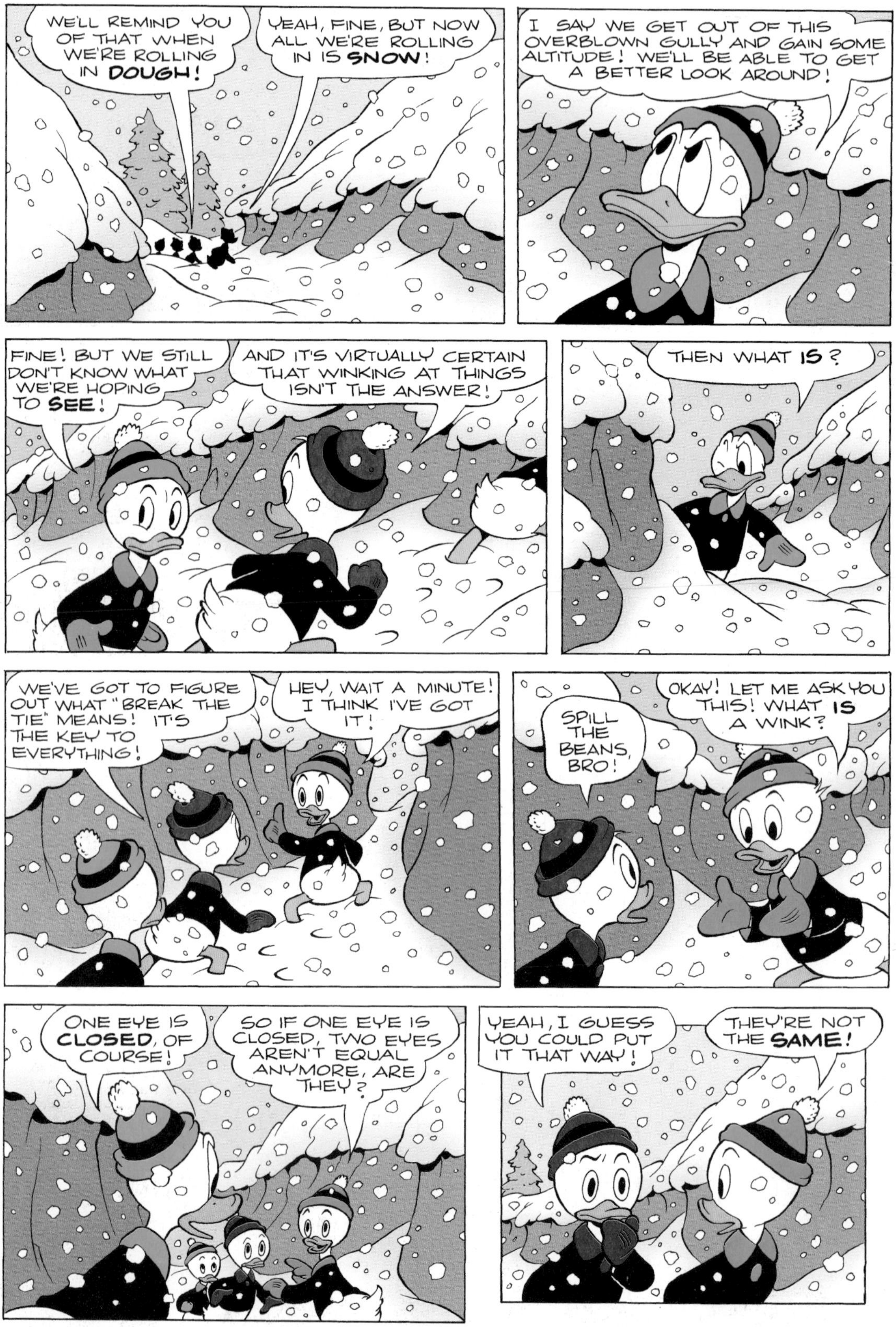
WE'LL REMIND YOU OF THAT WHEN WE'RE ROLLING IN DOUGH!
YEAH, FINE, BUT NOW ALL WE'RE ROLLING IN IS SNOW!
I SAY WE GET OUT OF THIS OVERBLOWN GULLY AND GAIN SOME ALTITUDE! WE'LL BE ABLE TO GET A BETTER LOOK AROUND!
FINE! BUT WE STILL DON'T KNOW WHAT WE'RE HOPING TO SEE!
AND IT'S VIRTUALLY CERTAIN THAT WINKING AT THINGS ISN'T THE ANSWER!
THEN WHAT IS?
WE'VE GOT TO FIGURE OUT WHAT "BREAK THE TIE" MEANS! IT'S THE KEY TO EVERYTHING!
HEY, WAIT A MINUTE! I THINK I'VE GOT IT!
SPILL THE BEANS, BRO!
OKAY! LET ME ASK YOU THIS! WHAT IS A WINK?
ONE EYE IS CLOSED, OF COURSE!
SO IF ONE EYE IS CLOSED, TWO EYES AREN'T EQUAL ANYMORE, ARE THEY?
YEAH, I GUESS YOU COULD PUT IT THAT WAY!
THEY'RE NOT THE SAME!

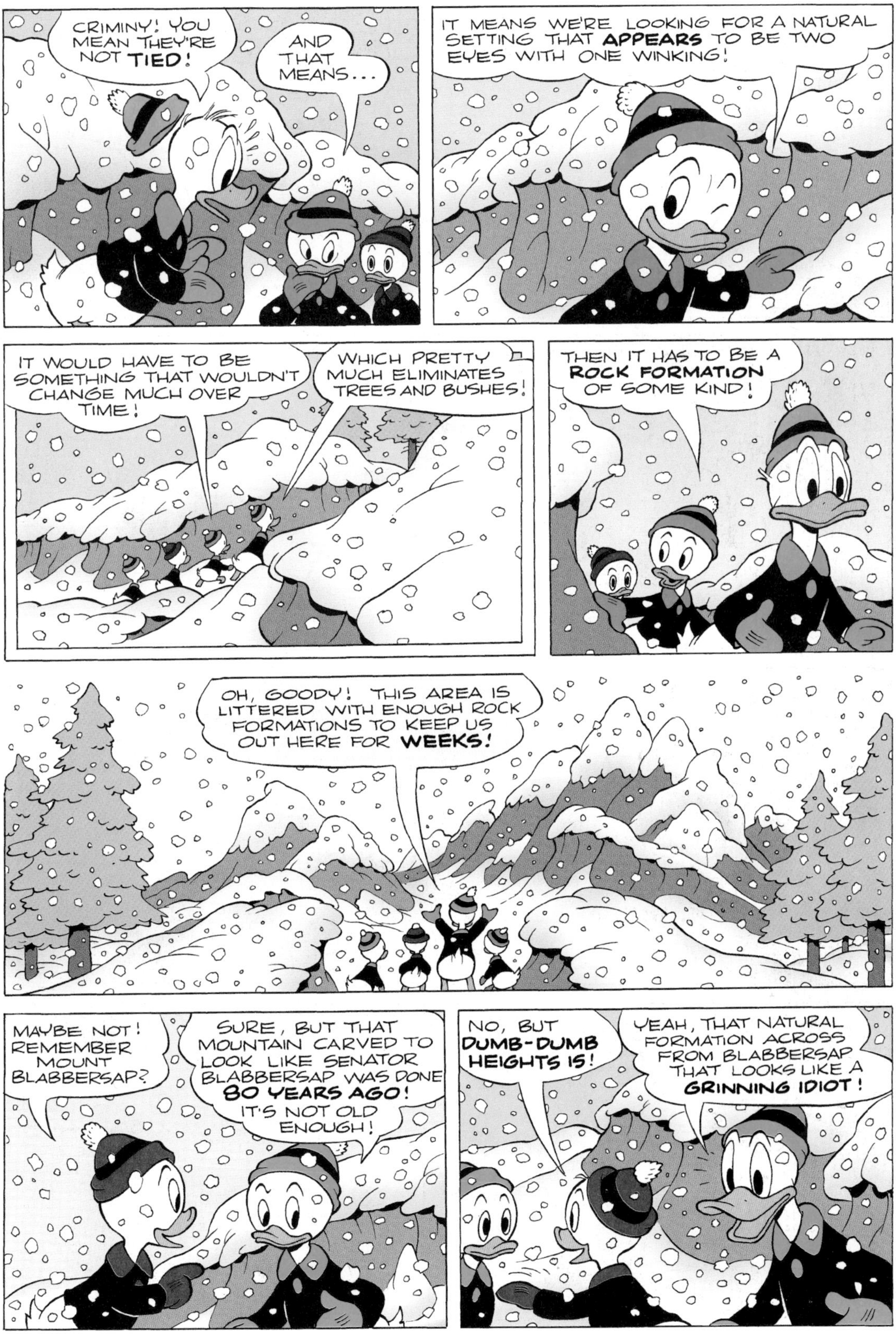

CRIMINY! YOU MEAN THEY'RE NOT **TIED**!
AND THAT MEANS...
IT MEANS WE'RE LOOKING FOR A NATURAL SETTING THAT **APPEARS** TO BE TWO EYES WITH ONE WINKING!
IT WOULD HAVE TO BE SOMETHING THAT WOULDN'T CHANGE MUCH OVER TIME!
WHICH PRETTY MUCH ELIMINATES TREES AND BUSHES!
THEN IT HAS TO BE A **ROCK FORMATION** OF SOME KIND!
OH, GOODY! THIS AREA IS LITTERED WITH ENOUGH ROCK FORMATIONS TO KEEP US OUT HERE FOR **WEEKS**!
MAYBE NOT! REMEMBER MOUNT BLABBERSAP?
SURE, BUT THAT MOUNTAIN CARVED TO LOOK LIKE SENATOR BLABBERSAP WAS DONE **80 YEARS AGO**! IT'S NOT OLD ENOUGH!
NO, BUT **DUMB-DUMB HEIGHTS IS**!
YEAH, THAT NATURAL FORMATION ACROSS FROM BLABBERSAP THAT LOOKS LIKE A **GRINNING IDIOT**!

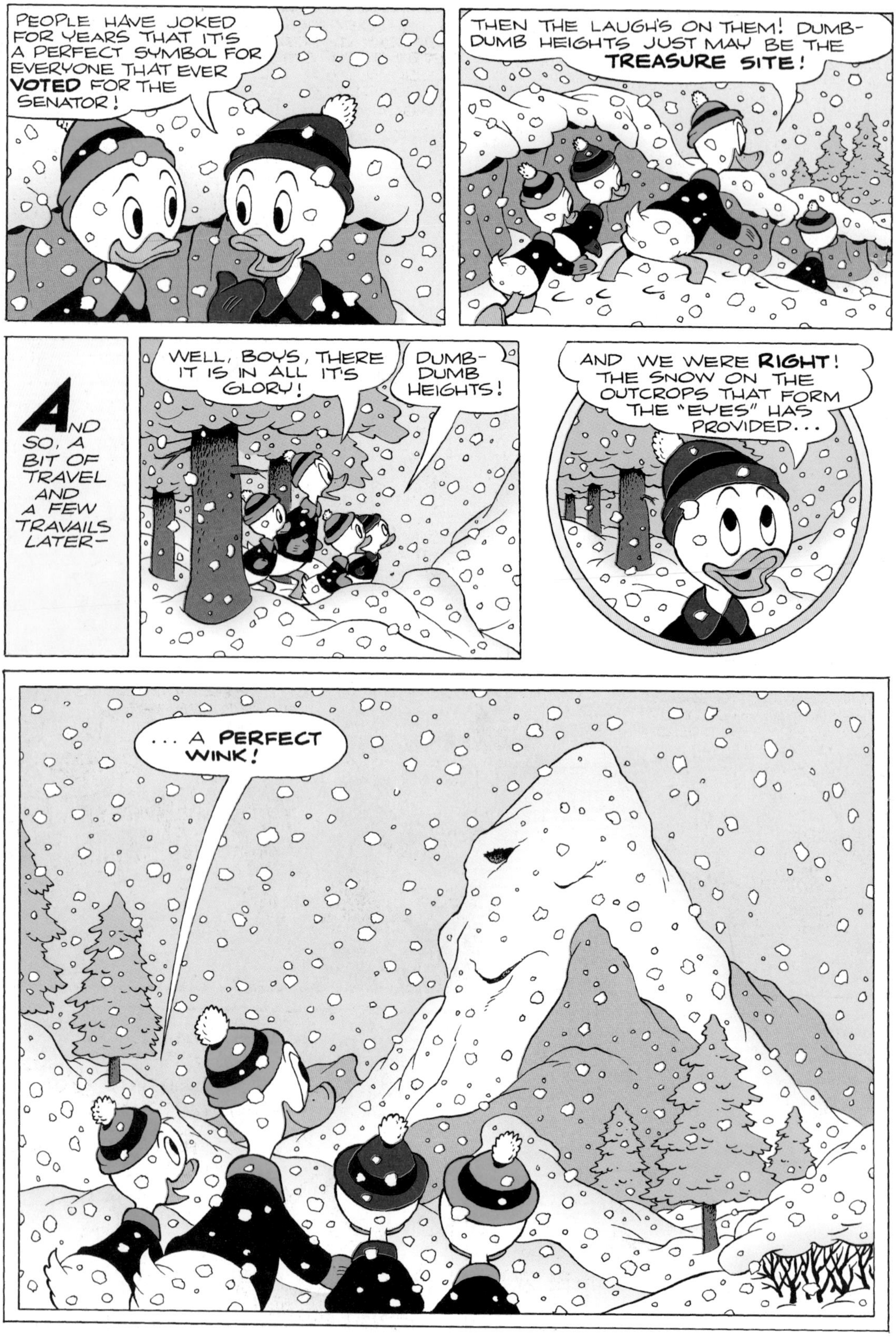

PEOPLE HAVE JOKED FOR YEARS THAT IT'S A PERFECT SYMBOL FOR EVERYONE THAT EVER **VOTED** FOR THE SENATOR!
THEN THE LAUGH'S ON THEM! DUMB-DUMB HEIGHTS JUST MAY BE THE **TREASURE SITE**!
AND SO, A BIT OF TRAVEL AND A FEW TRAVAILS LATER—
WELL, BOYS, THERE IT IS IN ALL IT'S GLORY!
DUMB-DUMB HEIGHTS!
AND WE WERE **RIGHT**! THE SNOW ON THE OUTCROPS THAT FORM THE "EYES" HAS PROVIDED...
... A **PERFECT WINK**!

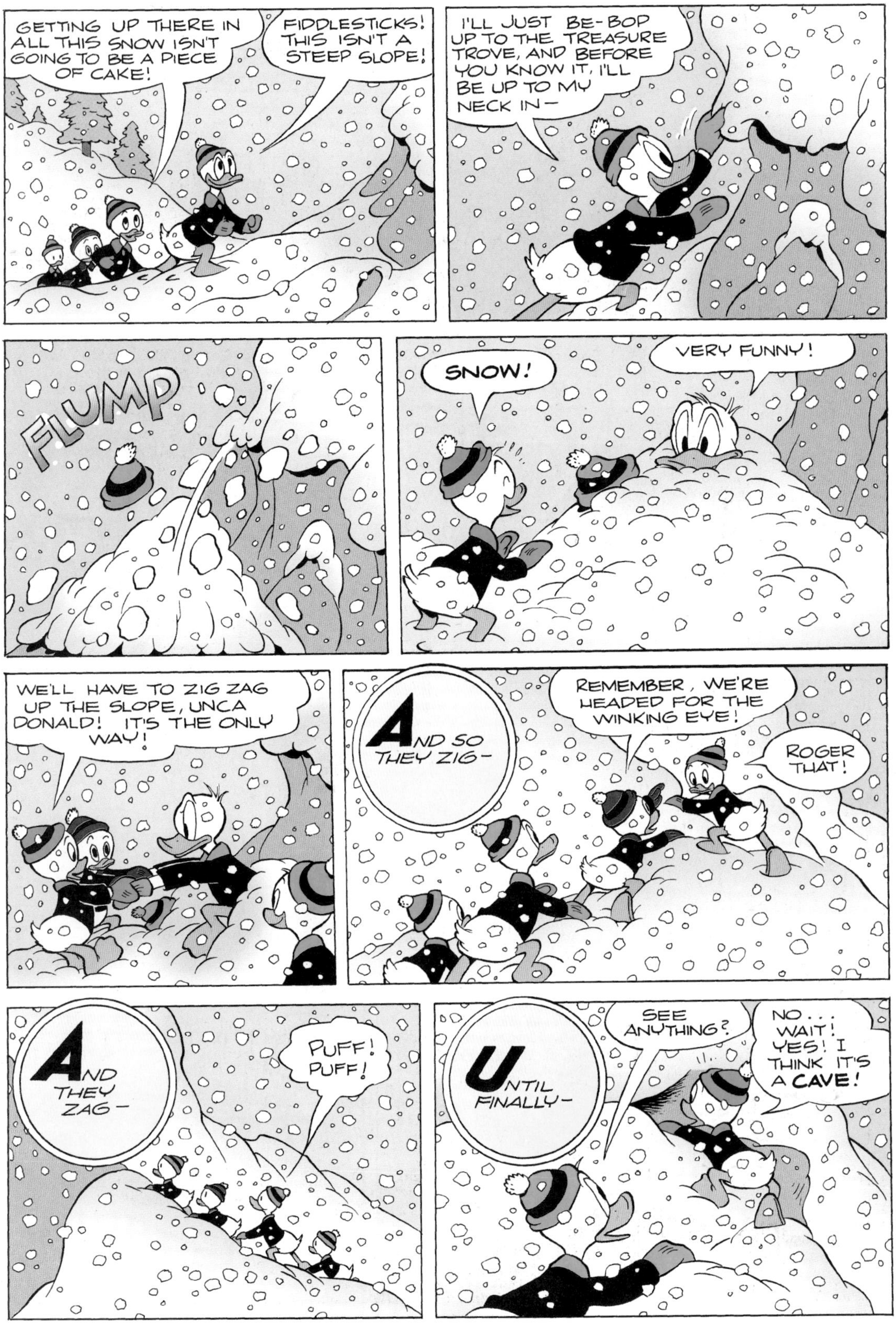
GETTING UP THERE IN ALL THIS SNOW ISN'T GOING TO BE A PIECE OF CAKE!
FIDDLESTICKS! THIS ISN'T A STEEP SLOPE!
I'LL JUST BE-BOP UP TO THE TREASURE TROVE, AND BEFORE YOU KNOW IT, I'LL BE UP TO MY NECK IN—
FLUMP
SNOW!
VERY FUNNY!
WE'LL HAVE TO ZIG ZAG UP THE SLOPE, UNCA DONALD! IT'S THE ONLY WAY!
AND SO THEY ZIG—
REMEMBER, WE'RE HEADED FOR THE WINKING EYE!
ROGER THAT!
AND THEY ZAG—
PUFF! PUFF!
UNTIL FINALLY—
SEE ANYTHING?
NO... WAIT! YES! I THINK IT'S A CAVE!

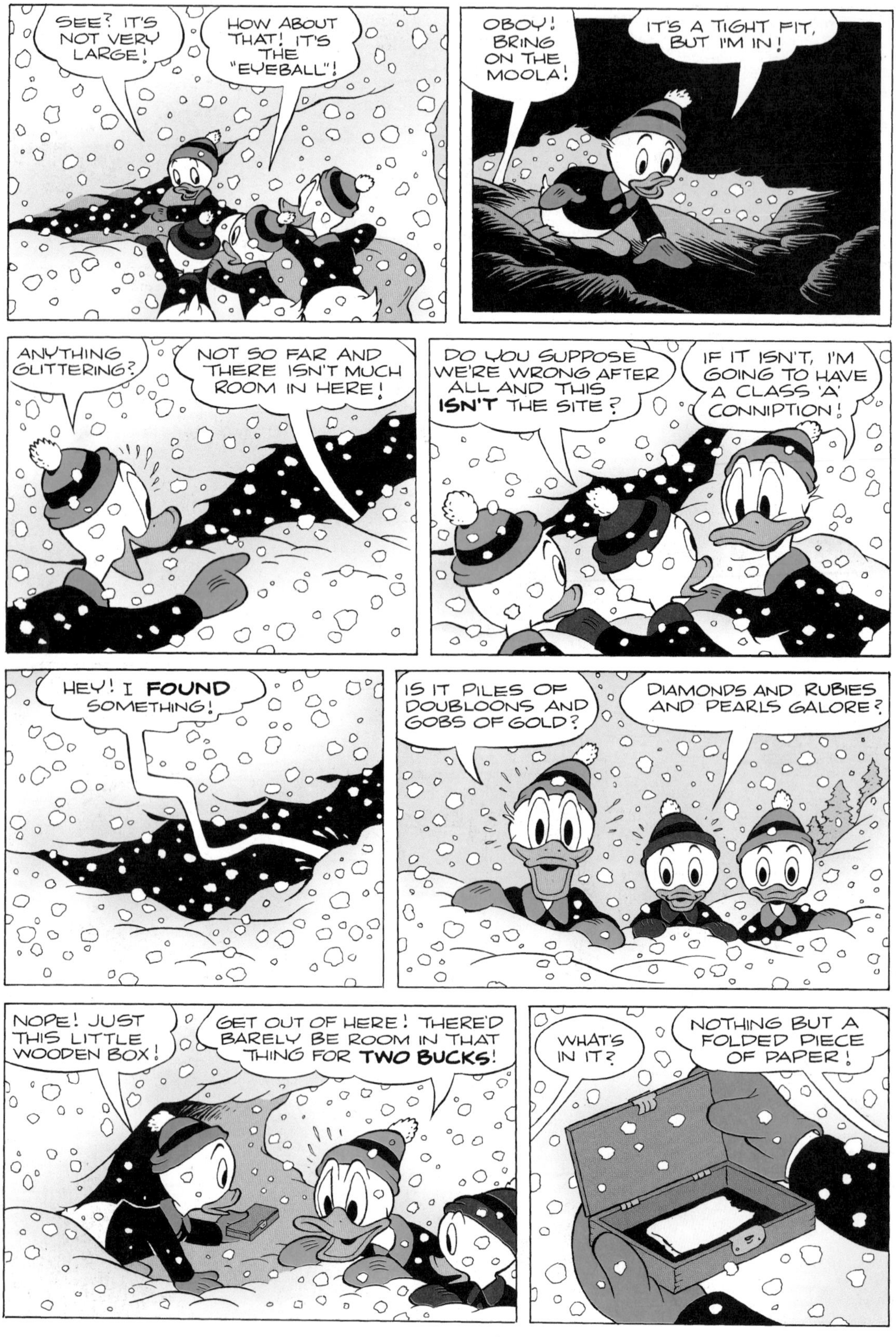
SEE? IT'S NOT VERY LARGE!
HOW ABOUT THAT! IT'S THE "EYEBALL"!
OBOY! BRING ON THE MOOLA!
IT'S A TIGHT FIT, BUT I'M IN!
ANYTHING GLITTERING?
NOT SO FAR AND THERE ISN'T MUCH ROOM IN HERE!
DO YOU SUPPOSE WE'RE WRONG AFTER ALL AND THIS **ISN'T** THE SITE?
IF IT ISN'T, I'M GOING TO HAVE A CLASS 'A' CONNIPTION!
HEY! I **FOUND** SOMETHING!
IS IT PILES OF DOUBLOONS AND GOBS OF GOLD?
DIAMONDS AND RUBIES AND PEARLS GALORE?
NOPE! JUST THIS LITTLE WOODEN BOX!
GET OUT OF HERE! THERE'D BARELY BE ROOM IN THAT THING FOR **TWO BUCKS**!
WHAT'S IN IT?
NOTHING BUT A FOLDED PIECE OF PAPER!

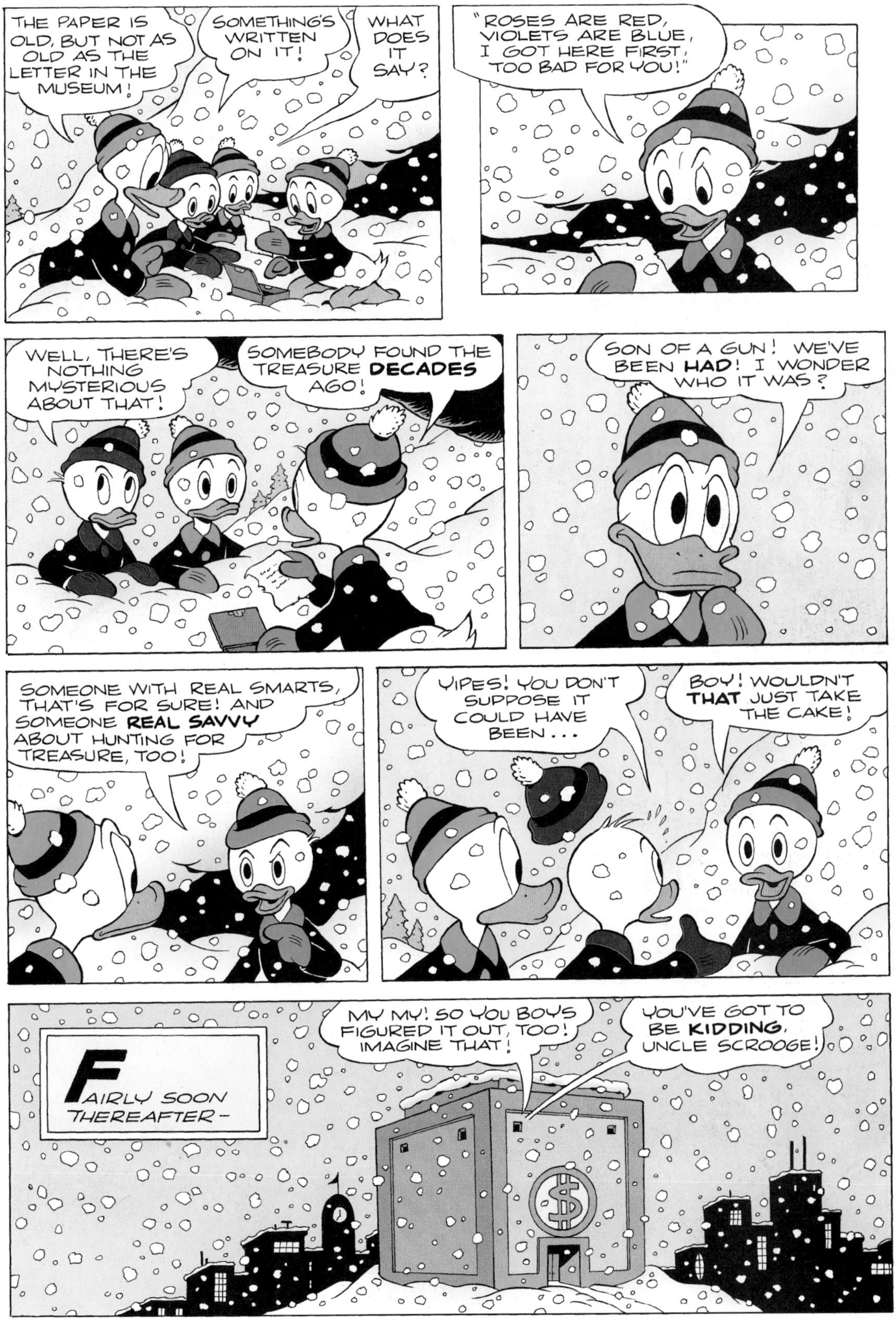
THE PAPER IS OLD, BUT NOT AS OLD AS THE LETTER IN THE MUSEUM!
SOMETHING'S WRITTEN ON IT!
WHAT DOES IT SAY?
"ROSES ARE RED, VIOLETS ARE BLUE, I GOT HERE FIRST, TOO BAD FOR YOU!"
WELL, THERE'S NOTHING MYSTERIOUS ABOUT THAT!
SOMEBODY FOUND THE TREASURE DECADES AGO!
SON OF A GUN! WE'VE BEEN HAD! I WONDER WHO IT WAS?
SOMEONE WITH REAL SMARTS, THAT'S FOR SURE! AND SOMEONE REAL SAVVY ABOUT HUNTING FOR TREASURE, TOO!
YIPES! YOU DON'T SUPPOSE IT COULD HAVE BEEN...
BOY! WOULDN'T THAT JUST TAKE THE CAKE!
FAIRLY SOON THEREAFTER-
MY MY! SO YOU BOYS FIGURED IT OUT, TOO! IMAGINE THAT!
YOU'VE GOT TO BE KIDDING, UNCLE SCROOGE!

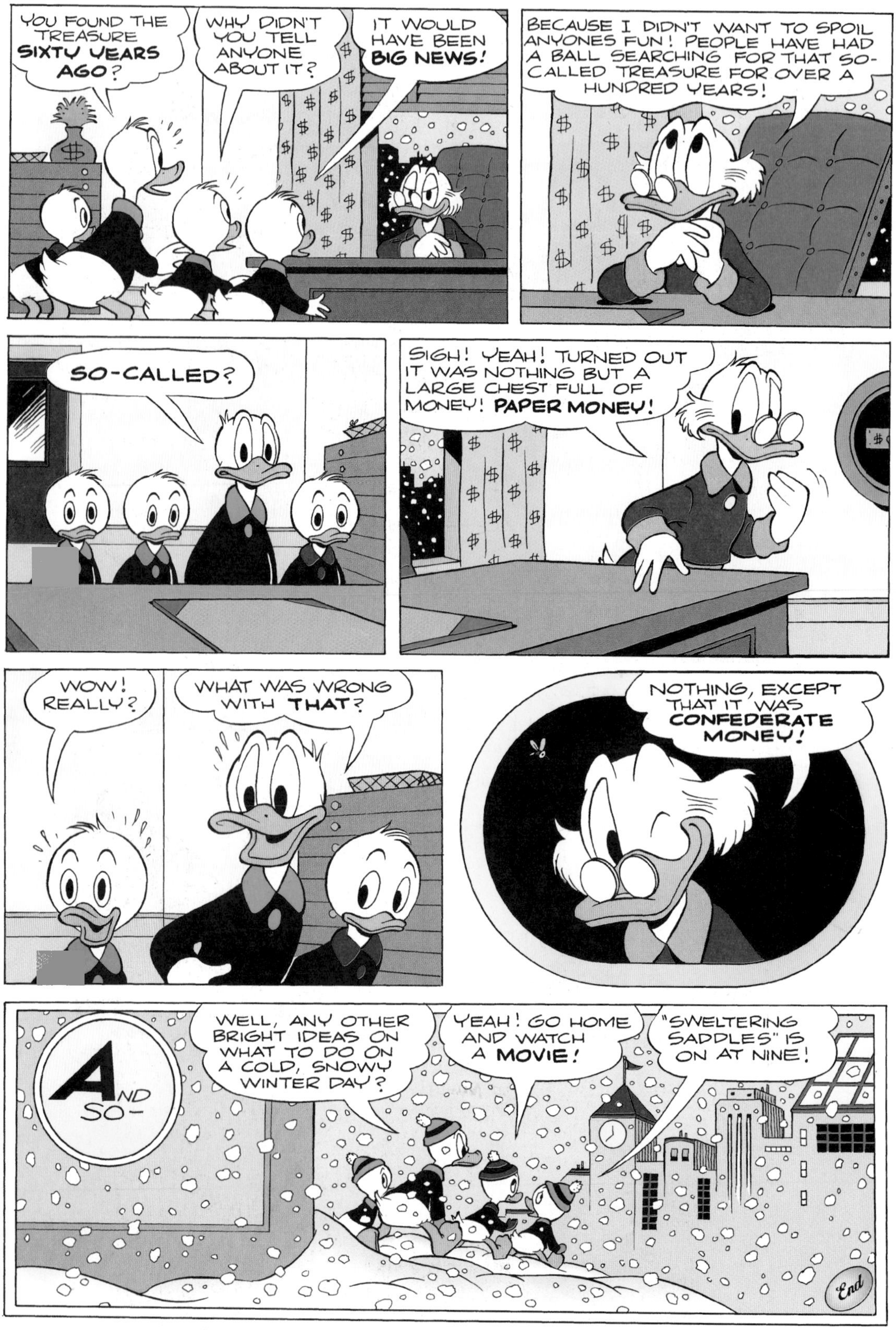
YOU FOUND THE TREASURE SIXTY YEARS AGO?
WHY DIDN'T YOU TELL ANYONE ABOUT IT?
IT WOULD HAVE BEEN BIG NEWS!
BECAUSE I DIDN'T WANT TO SPOIL ANYONES FUN! PEOPLE HAVE HAD A BALL SEARCHING FOR THAT SO-CALLED TREASURE FOR OVER A HUNDRED YEARS!
SO-CALLED?
SIGH! YEAH! TURNED OUT IT WAS NOTHING BUT A LARGE CHEST FULL OF MONEY! PAPER MONEY!
WOW! REALLY?
WHAT WAS WRONG WITH THAT?
NOTHING, EXCEPT THAT IT WAS CONFEDERATE MONEY!
AND SO-
WELL, ANY OTHER BRIGHT IDEAS ON WHAT TO DO ON A COLD, SNOWY WINTER DAY?
YEAH! GO HOME AND WATCH A MOVIE!
"SWELTERING SADDLES" IS ON AT NINE!
End

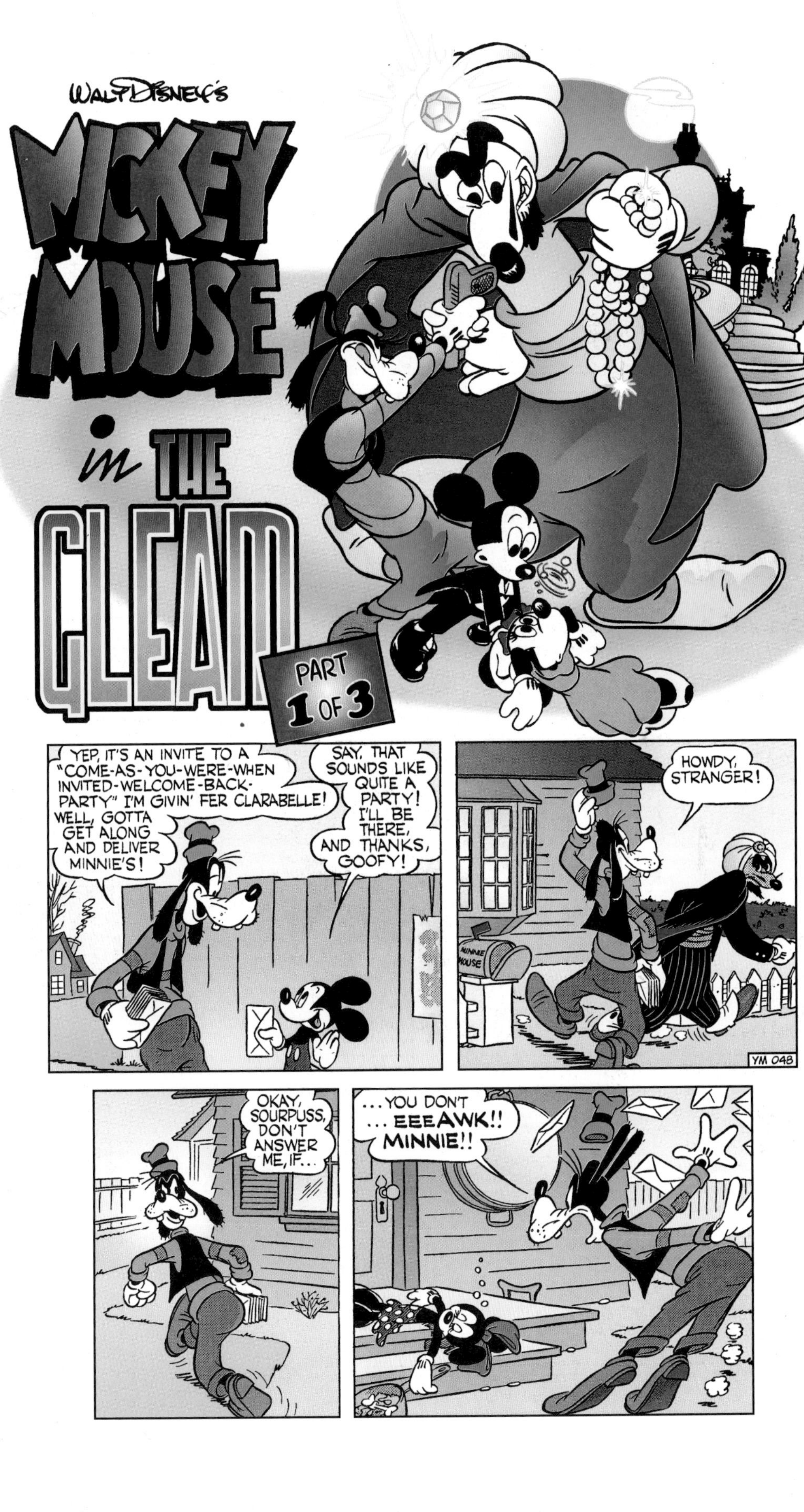
WALT DISNEY'S
MICKEY MOUSE
in THE GLEAM
PART 1 OF 3
YEP, IT'S AN INVITE TO A "COME-AS-YOU-WERE-WHEN INVITED-WELCOME-BACK-PARTY" I'M GIVIN' FER CLARABELLE!
WELL, GOTTA GET ALONG AND DELIVER MINNIE'S!
SAY, THAT SOUNDS LIKE QUITE A PARTY! I'LL BE THERE, AND THANKS, GOOFY!
HOWDY, STRANGER!
MINNIE MOUSE
YM 048
OKAY, SOURPUSS, DON'T ANSWER ME, IF...
...YOU DON'T ...EEEAWK!! MINNIE!!

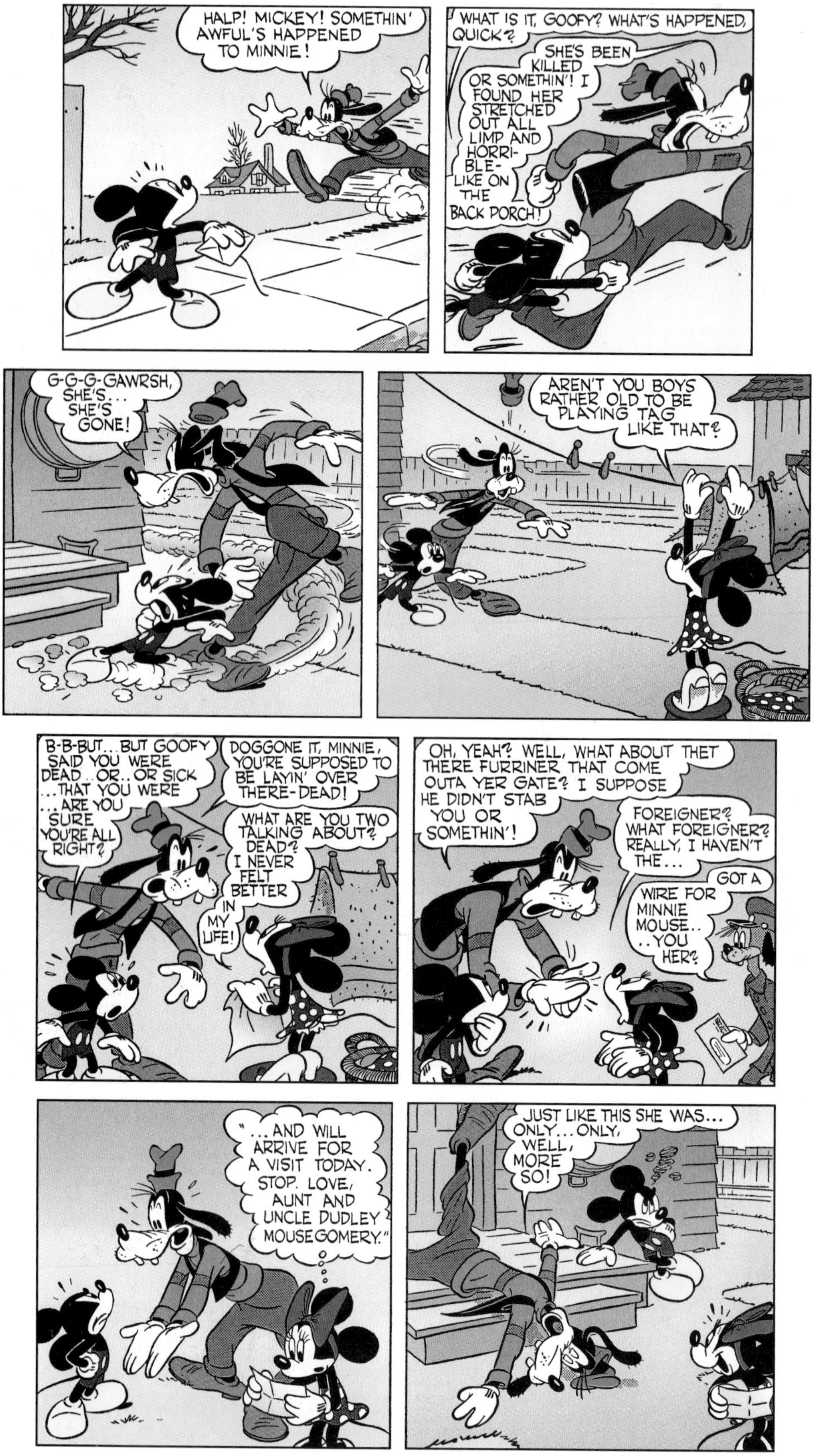
HALP! MICKEY! SOMETHIN' AWFUL'S HAPPENED TO MINNIE!
WHAT IS IT, GOOFY? WHAT'S HAPPENED, QUICK?
SHE'S BEEN KILLED OR SOMETHIN'! I FOUND HER STRETCHED OUT ALL LIMP AND HORRI-BLE-LIKE ON THE BACK PORCH!
G-G-G-GAWRSH, SHE'S... SHE'S GONE!
AREN'T YOU BOYS RATHER OLD TO BE PLAYING TAG LIKE THAT?
B-B-BUT... BUT GOOFY SAID YOU WERE DEAD.. OR.. OR SICK ...THAT YOU WERE ...ARE YOU SURE YOU'RE ALL RIGHT?
DOGGONE IT, MINNIE, YOU'RE SUPPOSED TO BE LAYIN' OVER THERE-DEAD!
WHAT ARE YOU TWO TALKING ABOUT? DEAD? I NEVER FELT BETTER IN MY LIFE!
OH, YEAH? WELL, WHAT ABOUT THET THERE FURRINER THAT COME OUTA YER GATE? I SUPPOSE HE DIDN'T STAB YOU OR SOMETHIN'!
FOREIGNER? WHAT FOREIGNER? REALLY, I HAVEN'T THE...
GOT A WIRE FOR MINNIE MOUSE.. ..YOU HER?
"...AND WILL ARRIVE FOR A VISIT TODAY. STOP. LOVE, AUNT AND UNCLE DUDLEY MOUSEGOMERY."
JUST LIKE THIS SHE WAS... ONLY... ONLY, WELL, MORE SO!

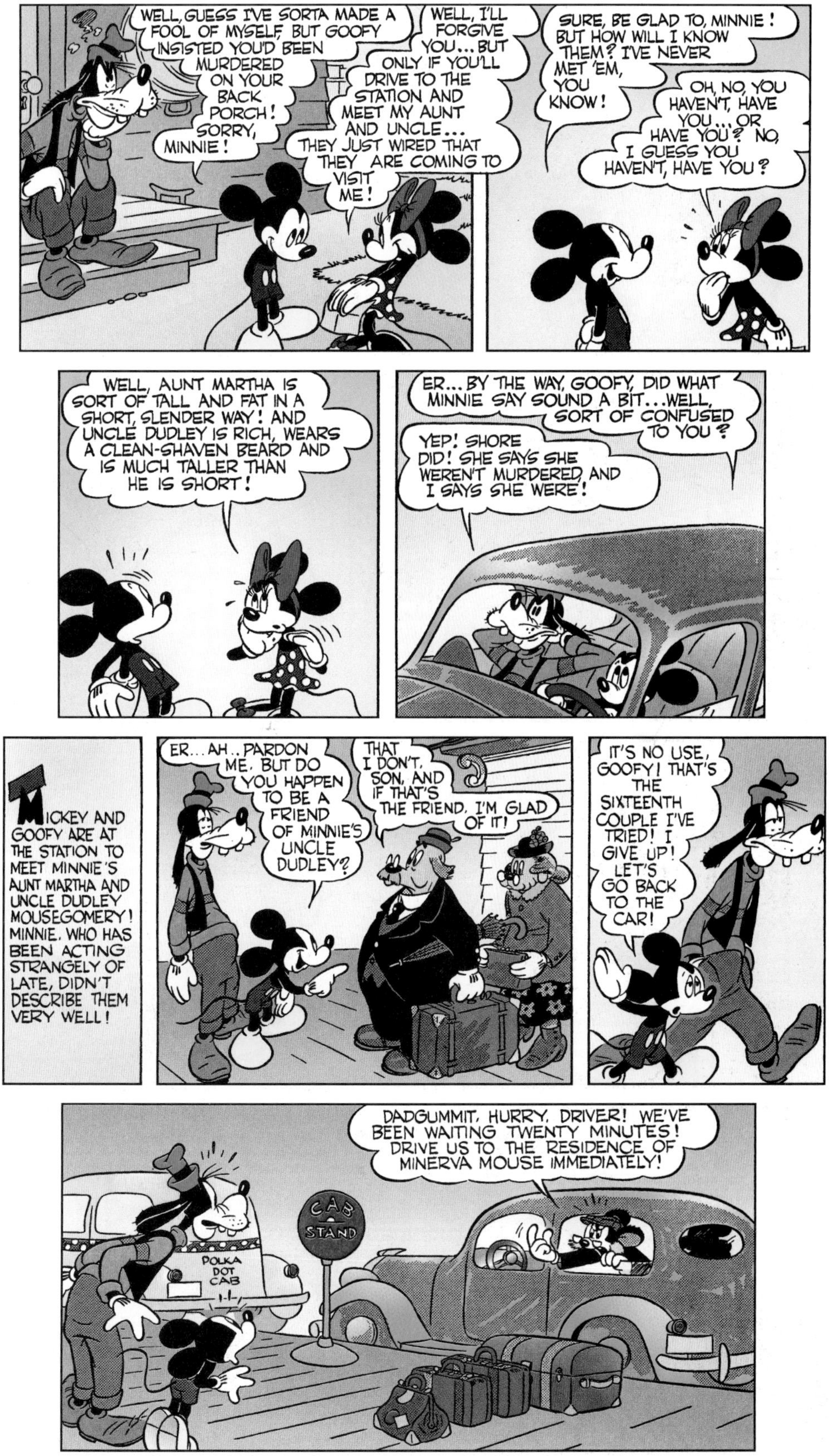
WELL, GUESS I'VE SORTA MADE A FOOL OF MYSELF, BUT GOOFY INSISTED YOU'D BEEN MURDERED ON YOUR BACK PORCH! SORRY, MINNIE!
WELL, I'LL FORGIVE YOU... BUT ONLY IF YOU'LL DRIVE TO THE STATION AND MEET MY AUNT AND UNCLE... THEY JUST WIRED THAT THEY ARE COMING TO VISIT ME!
SURE, BE GLAD TO, MINNIE! BUT HOW WILL I KNOW THEM? I'VE NEVER MET 'EM, YOU KNOW!
OH, NO, YOU HAVEN'T, HAVE YOU... OR HAVE YOU? NO, I GUESS YOU HAVEN'T, HAVE YOU?
WELL, AUNT MARTHA IS SORT OF TALL AND FAT IN A SHORT, SLENDER WAY! AND UNCLE DUDLEY IS RICH, WEARS A CLEAN-SHAVEN BEARD AND IS MUCH TALLER THAN HE IS SHORT!
ER... BY THE WAY, GOOFY, DID WHAT MINNIE SAY SOUND A BIT...WELL, SORT OF CONFUSED TO YOU?
YEP! SHORE DID! SHE SAYS SHE WEREN'T MURDERED, AND I SAYS SHE WERE!
MICKEY AND GOOFY ARE AT THE STATION TO MEET MINNIE'S AUNT MARTHA AND UNCLE DUDLEY MOUSEGOMERY! MINNIE, WHO HAS BEEN ACTING STRANGELY OF LATE, DIDN'T DESCRIBE THEM VERY WELL!
ER... AH.. PARDON ME, BUT DO YOU HAPPEN TO BE A FRIEND OF MINNIE'S UNCLE DUDLEY?
THAT I DON'T, SON, AND IF THAT'S THE FRIEND, I'M GLAD OF IT!
IT'S NO USE, GOOFY! THAT'S THE SIXTEENTH COUPLE I'VE TRIED! I GIVE UP! LET'S GO BACK TO THE CAR!
DADGUMMIT, HURRY, DRIVER! WE'VE BEEN WAITING TWENTY MINUTES! DRIVE US TO THE RESIDENCE OF MINERVA MOUSE IMMEDIATELY!
CAB STAND
POLKA DOT CAB

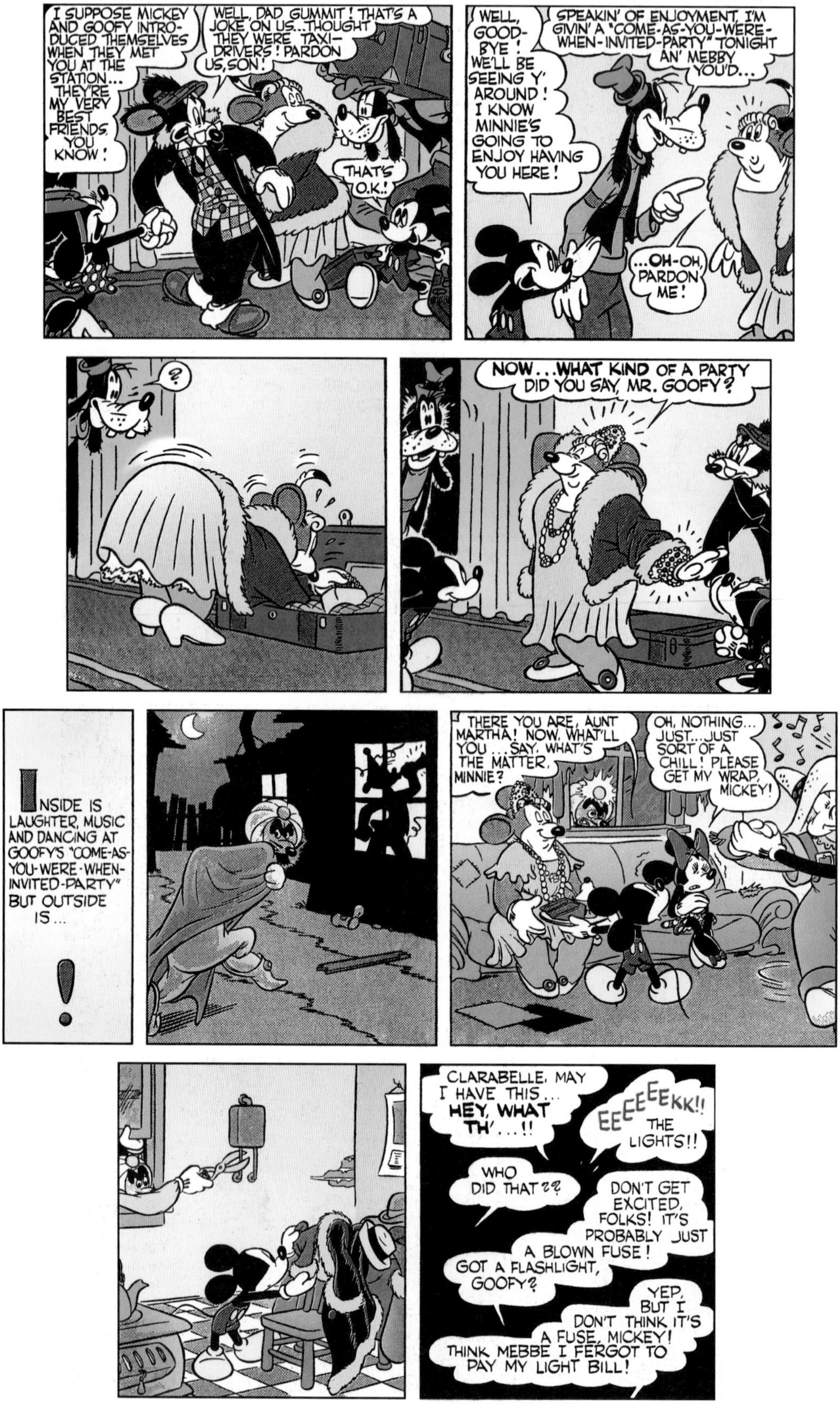
I SUPPOSE MICKEY AND GOOFY INTRODUCED THEMSELVES WHEN THEY MET YOU AT THE STATION... THEY'RE MY VERY BEST FRIENDS, YOU KNOW!
WELL, DAD GUMMIT! THAT'S A JOKE ON US...THOUGHT THEY WERE TAXI-DRIVERS! PARDON US, SON!
THAT'S O.K.!
WELL, GOOD-BYE! WE'LL BE SEEING Y' AROUND! I KNOW MINNIE'S GOING TO ENJOY HAVING YOU HERE!
SPEAKIN' OF ENJOYMENT, I'M GIVIN' A "COME-AS-YOU-WERE-WHEN-INVITED-PARTY" TONIGHT AN' MEBBY YOU'D...
...OH-OH, PARDON ME!
?
NOW...WHAT KIND OF A PARTY DID YOU SAY, MR. GOOFY?
INSIDE IS LAUGHTER, MUSIC AND DANCING AT GOOFY'S "COME-AS-YOU-WERE-WHEN-INVITED-PARTY" BUT OUTSIDE IS...
!
THERE YOU ARE, AUNT MARTHA! NOW, WHAT'LL YOU ...SAY, WHAT'S THE MATTER, MINNIE?
OH, NOTHING... JUST...JUST SORT OF A CHILL! PLEASE GET MY WRAP, MICKEY!
CLARABELLE, MAY I HAVE THIS... HEY, WHAT TH'...!!
EEEEEEKK!! THE LIGHTS!!
WHO DID THAT ??
DON'T GET EXCITED, FOLKS! IT'S PROBABLY JUST A BLOWN FUSE!
GOT A FLASHLIGHT, GOOFY?
YEP, BUT I DON'T THINK IT'S A FUSE, MICKEY! THINK MEBBE I FERGOT TO PAY MY LIGHT BILL!

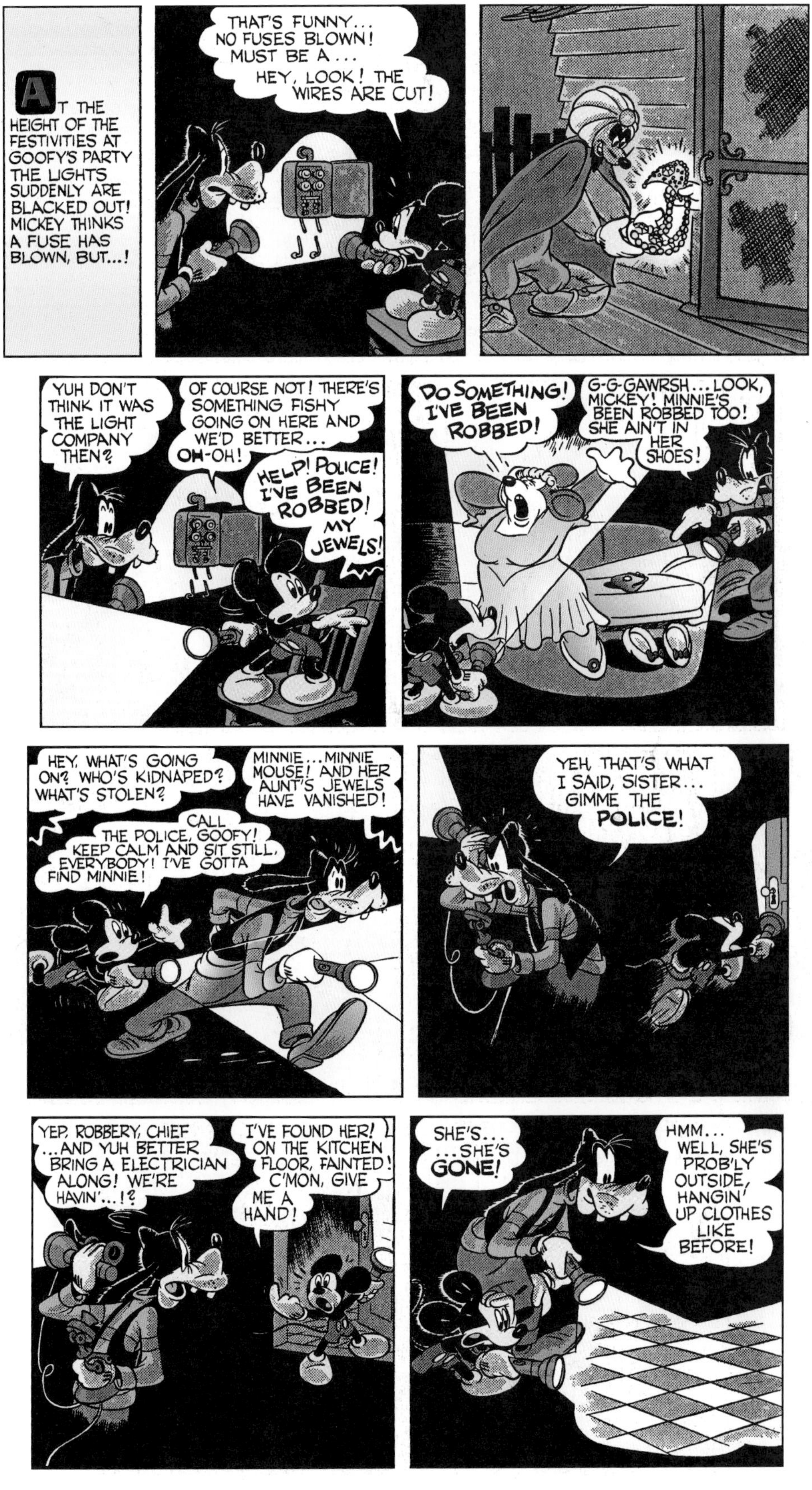
AT THE HEIGHT OF THE FESTIVITIES AT GOOFY'S PARTY THE LIGHTS SUDDENLY ARE BLACKED OUT! MICKEY THINKS A FUSE HAS BLOWN, BUT...!
THAT'S FUNNY... NO FUSES BLOWN! MUST BE A...
HEY, LOOK! THE WIRES ARE CUT!
YUH DON'T THINK IT WAS THE LIGHT COMPANY THEN?
OF COURSE NOT! THERE'S SOMETHING FISHY GOING ON HERE AND WE'D BETTER... OH-OH!
HELP! POLICE! I'VE BEEN ROBBED! MY JEWELS!
DO SOMETHING! I'VE BEEN ROBBED!
G-G-GAWRSH... LOOK, MICKEY! MINNIE'S BEEN ROBBED TOO! SHE AIN'T IN HER SHOES!
HEY, WHAT'S GOING ON? WHO'S KIDNAPED? WHAT'S STOLEN?
MINNIE... MINNIE MOUSE! AND HER AUNT'S JEWELS HAVE VANISHED!
CALL THE POLICE, GOOFY! KEEP CALM AND SIT STILL, EVERYBODY! I'VE GOTTA FIND MINNIE!
YEH, THAT'S WHAT I SAID, SISTER... GIMME THE POLICE!
YEP, ROBBERY, CHIEF ...AND YUH BETTER BRING A ELECTRICIAN ALONG! WE'RE HAVIN'...!?
I'VE FOUND HER! ON THE KITCHEN FLOOR, FAINTED! C'MON, GIVE ME A HAND!
SHE'S... ...SHE'S GONE!
HMM... WELL, SHE'S PROB'LY OUTSIDE, HANGIN' UP CLOTHES LIKE BEFORE!

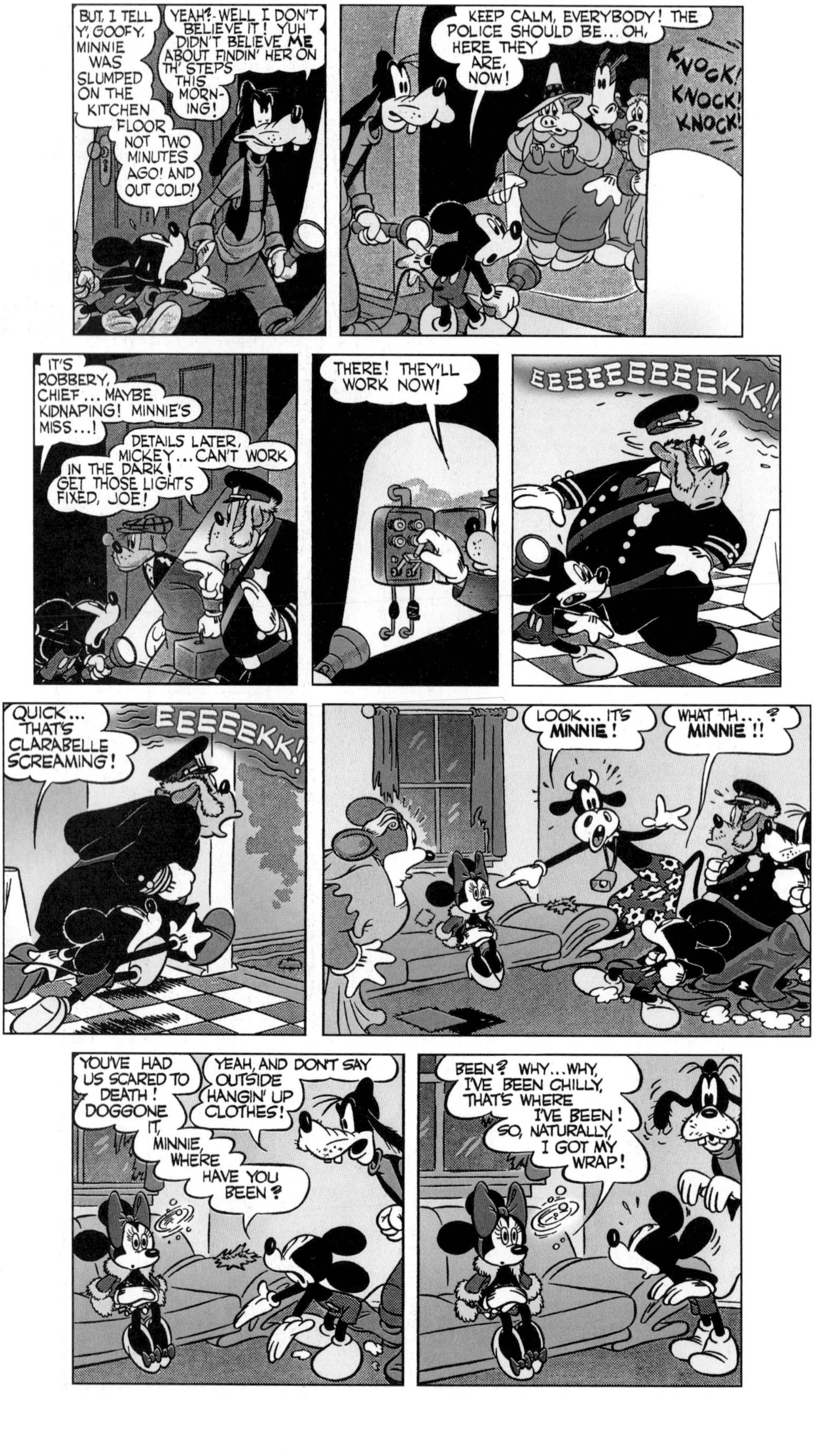
BUT, I TELL Y', GOOFY, MINNIE WAS SLUMPED ON THE KITCHEN FLOOR NOT TWO MINUTES AGO! AND OUT COLD!
YEAH?-WELL I DON'T BELIEVE IT! YUH DIDN'T BELIEVE ME ABOUT FINDIN' HER ON TH' STEPS THIS MORNING!
KEEP CALM, EVERYBODY! THE POLICE SHOULD BE...OH, HERE THEY ARE, NOW!
KNOCK! KNOCK! KNOCK!
IT'S ROBBERY, CHIEF... MAYBE KIDNAPING! MINNIE'S MISS...!
DETAILS LATER, MICKEY... CAN'T WORK IN THE DARK! GET THOSE LIGHTS FIXED, JOE!
THERE! THEY'LL WORK NOW!
EEEEEEEEEEKK!!
QUICK... THAT'S CLARABELLE SCREAMING!
EEEEEKK!!
LOOK... IT'S MINNIE!
WHAT TH...? MINNIE!!
YOU'VE HAD US SCARED TO DEATH! DOGGONE IT, MINNIE, WHERE HAVE YOU BEEN?
YEAH, AND DON'T SAY OUTSIDE HANGIN' UP CLOTHES!
BEEN? WHY...WHY, I'VE BEEN CHILLY, THAT'S WHERE I'VE BEEN! SO, NATURALLY, I GOT MY WRAP!

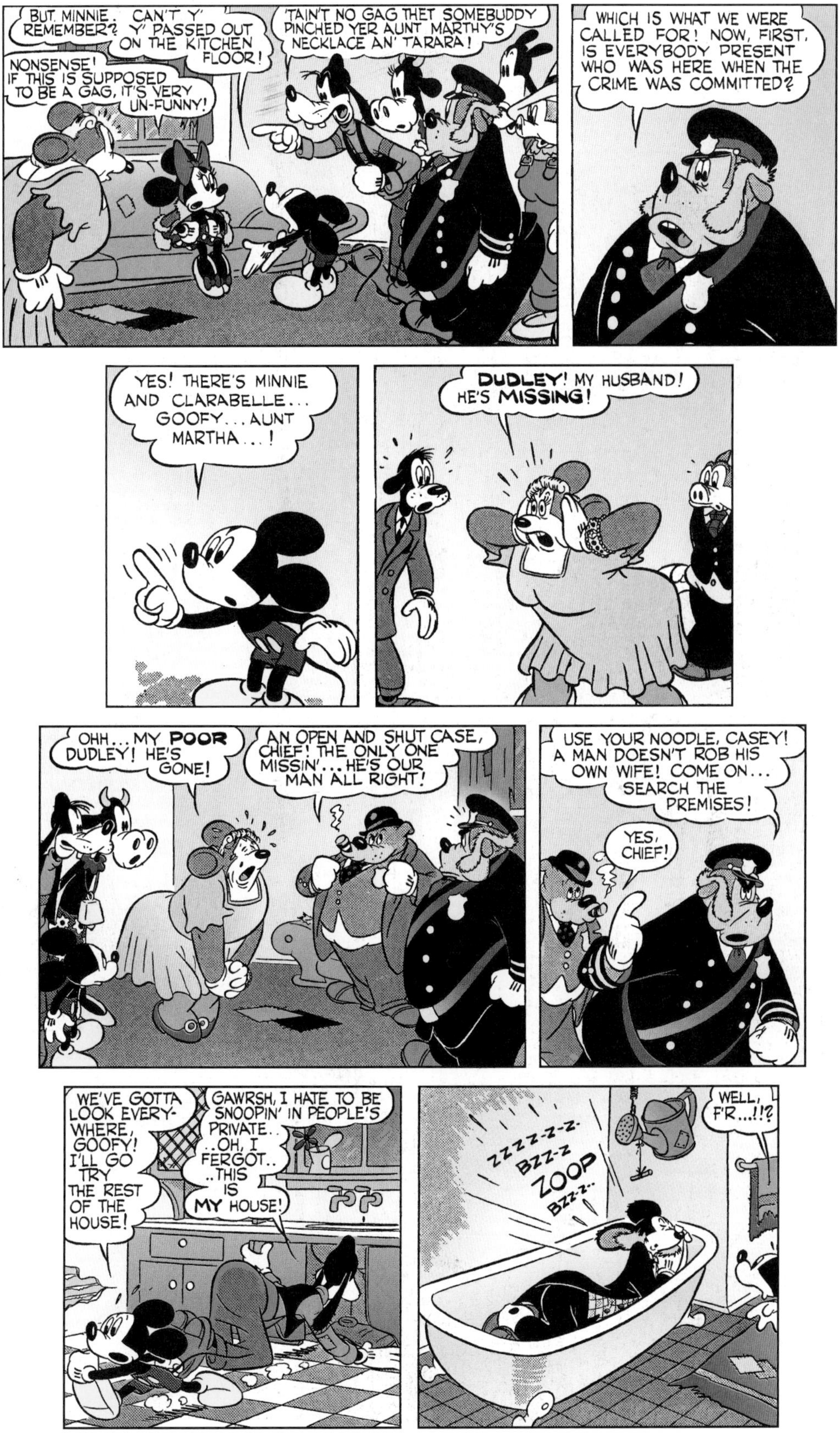

BUT MINNIE, CAN'T Y' REMEMBER? Y' PASSED OUT ON THE KITCHEN FLOOR!
NONSENSE! IF THIS IS SUPPOSED TO BE A GAG, IT'S VERY UN-FUNNY!
'TAIN'T NO GAG THET SOMEBUDDY PINCHED YER AUNT MARTHY'S NECKLACE AN' TARARA!
WHICH IS WHAT WE WERE CALLED FOR! NOW, FIRST, IS EVERYBODY PRESENT WHO WAS HERE WHEN THE CRIME WAS COMMITTED?
YES! THERE'S MINNIE AND CLARABELLE... GOOFY... AUNT MARTHA...!
DUDLEY! MY HUSBAND! HE'S MISSING!
OHH... MY POOR DUDLEY! HE'S GONE!
AN OPEN AND SHUT CASE, CHIEF! THE ONLY ONE MISSIN'... HE'S OUR MAN ALL RIGHT!
USE YOUR NOODLE, CASEY! A MAN DOESN'T ROB HIS OWN WIFE! COME ON... SEARCH THE PREMISES!
YES, CHIEF!
WE'VE GOTTA LOOK EVERYWHERE, GOOFY! I'LL GO TRY THE REST OF THE HOUSE!
GAWRSH, I HATE TO BE SNOOPIN' IN PEOPLE'S PRIVATE.. ..OH, I FERGOT.. ..THIS IS MY HOUSE!
ZZZZ-Z-Z-Z- BZZ-Z ZOOP BZZ-Z..
WELL, F'R...!!?

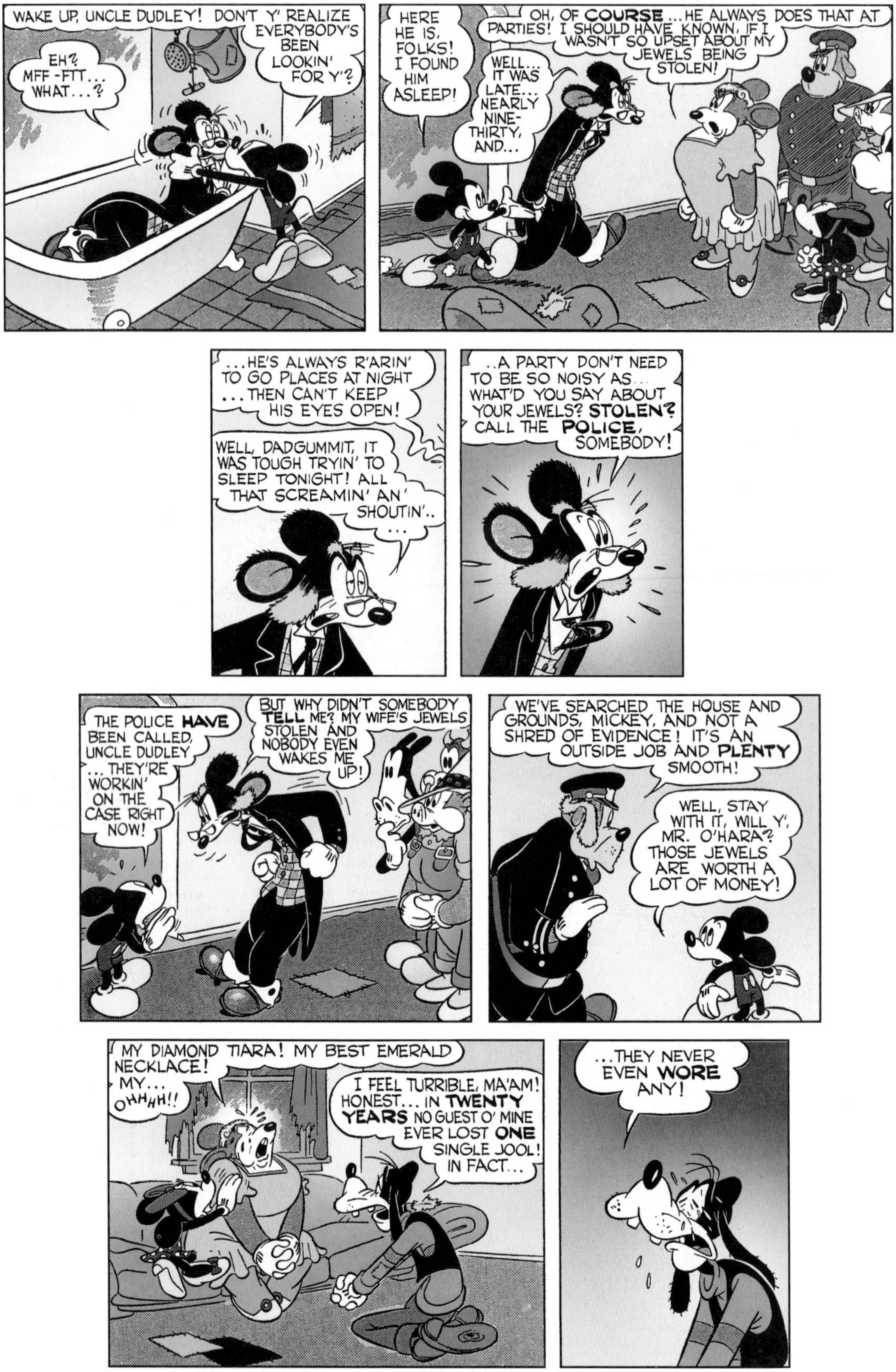
WAKE UP, UNCLE DUDLEY! DON'T Y' REALIZE EVERYBODY'S BEEN LOOKIN' FOR Y'?
EH? MFF -FTT... WHAT...?
HERE HE IS, FOLKS! I FOUND HIM ASLEEP!
OH, OF COURSE... HE ALWAYS DOES THAT AT PARTIES! I SHOULD HAVE KNOWN, IF I WASN'T SO UPSET ABOUT MY JEWELS BEING STOLEN!
WELL... IT WAS LATE... NEARLY NINE-THIRTY, AND...
...HE'S ALWAYS R'ARIN' TO GO PLACES AT NIGHT ...THEN CAN'T KEEP HIS EYES OPEN!
WELL, DADGUMMIT, IT WAS TOUGH TRYIN' TO SLEEP TONIGHT! ALL THAT SCREAMIN' AN' SHOUTIN'.. ...
..A PARTY DON'T NEED TO BE SO NOISY AS... WHAT'D YOU SAY ABOUT YOUR JEWELS? STOLEN? CALL THE POLICE, SOMEBODY!
THE POLICE HAVE BEEN CALLED, UNCLE DUDLEY ... THEY'RE WORKIN' ON THE CASE RIGHT NOW!
BUT WHY DIDN'T SOMEBODY TELL ME? MY WIFE'S JEWELS STOLEN AND NOBODY EVEN WAKES ME UP!
WE'VE SEARCHED THE HOUSE AND GROUNDS, MICKEY, AND NOT A SHRED OF EVIDENCE! IT'S AN OUTSIDE JOB AND PLENTY SMOOTH!
WELL, STAY WITH IT, WILL Y', MR. O'HARA? THOSE JEWELS ARE WORTH A LOT OF MONEY!
MY DIAMOND TIARA! MY BEST EMERALD NECKLACE! MY... OHHHH!!
I FEEL TURRIBLE, MA'AM! HONEST... IN TWENTY YEARS NO GUEST O' MINE EVER LOST ONE SINGLE JOOL! IN FACT...
...THEY NEVER EVEN WORE ANY!

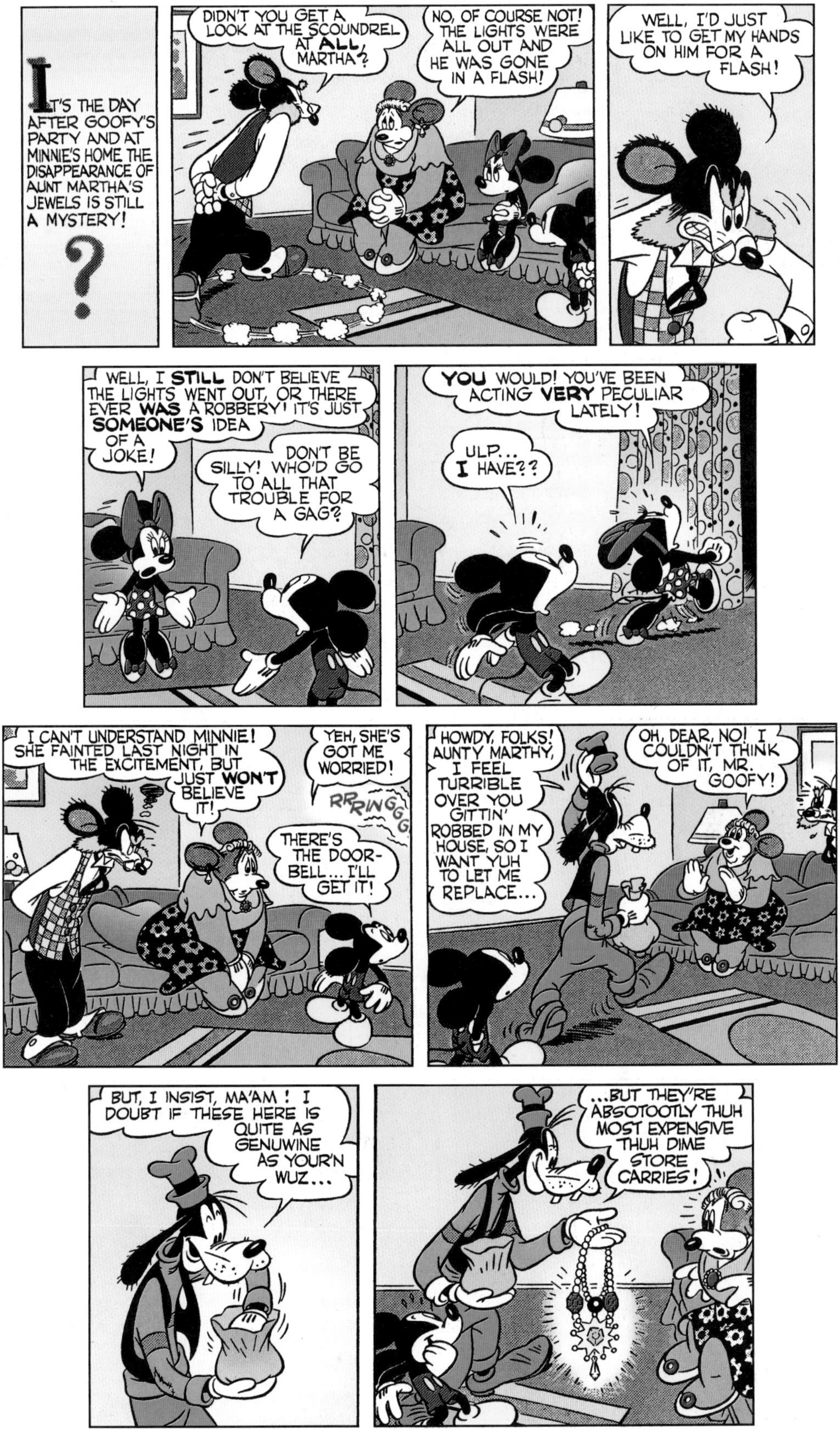
IT'S THE DAY AFTER GOOFY'S PARTY AND AT MINNIE'S HOME THE DISAPPEARANCE OF AUNT MARTHA'S JEWELS IS STILL A MYSTERY!
?
DIDN'T YOU GET A LOOK AT THE SCOUNDREL AT ALL, MARTHA?
NO, OF COURSE NOT! THE LIGHTS WERE ALL OUT AND HE WAS GONE IN A FLASH!
WELL, I'D JUST LIKE TO GET MY HANDS ON HIM FOR A FLASH!
WELL, I STILL DON'T BELIEVE THE LIGHTS WENT OUT, OR THERE EVER WAS A ROBBERY! IT'S JUST SOMEONE'S IDEA OF A JOKE!
DON'T BE SILLY! WHO'D GO TO ALL THAT TROUBLE FOR A GAG?
YOU WOULD! YOU'VE BEEN ACTING VERY PECULIAR LATELY!
ULP... I HAVE??
I CAN'T UNDERSTAND MINNIE! SHE FAINTED LAST NIGHT IN THE EXCITEMENT, BUT JUST WON'T BELIEVE IT!
YEH, SHE'S GOT ME WORRIED!
RRRINGGG
THERE'S THE DOOR-BELL... I'LL GET IT!
HOWDY, FOLKS! AUNTY MARTHY, I FEEL TURRIBLE OVER YOU GITTIN' ROBBED IN MY HOUSE, SO I WANT YUH TO LET ME REPLACE...
OH, DEAR, NO! I COULDN'T THINK OF IT, MR. GOOFY!
BUT, I INSIST, MA'AM! I DOUBT IF THESE HERE IS QUITE AS GENUWINE AS YOUR'N WUZ...
...BUT THEY'RE ABSOTOOTLY THUH MOST EXPENSIVE THUH DIME STORE CARRIES!

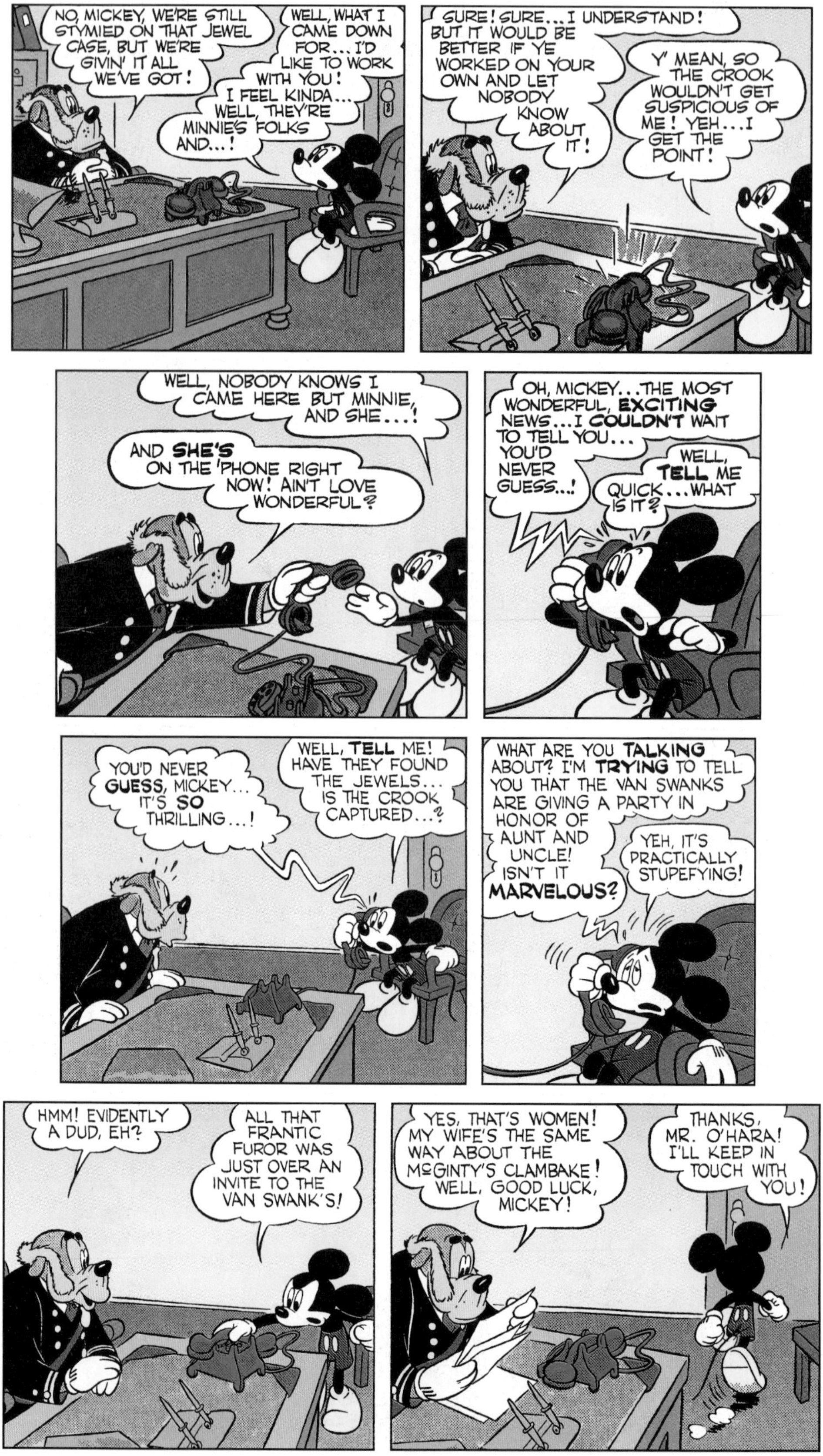

NO, MICKEY, WE'RE STILL STYMIED ON THAT JEWEL CASE, BUT WE'RE GIVIN' IT ALL WE'VE GOT!
WELL, WHAT I CAME DOWN FOR... I'D LIKE TO WORK WITH YOU! I FEEL KINDA... WELL, THEY'RE MINNIE'S FOLKS AND...!
SURE! SURE... I UNDERSTAND! BUT IT WOULD BE BETTER IF YE WORKED ON YOUR OWN AND LET NOBODY KNOW ABOUT IT!
Y' MEAN, SO THE CROOK WOULDN'T GET SUSPICIOUS OF ME! YEH... I GET THE POINT!
WELL, NOBODY KNOWS I CAME HERE BUT MINNIE, AND SHE...!
AND SHE'S ON THE 'PHONE RIGHT NOW! AIN'T LOVE WONDERFUL?
OH, MICKEY... THE MOST WONDERFUL, EXCITING NEWS... I COULDN'T WAIT TO TELL YOU... YOU'D NEVER GUESS...!
WELL, TELL ME QUICK... WHAT IS IT?
YOU'D NEVER GUESS, MICKEY... IT'S SO THRILLING...!
WELL, TELL ME! HAVE THEY FOUND THE JEWELS... IS THE CROOK CAPTURED...?
WHAT ARE YOU TALKING ABOUT? I'M TRYING TO TELL YOU THAT THE VAN SWANKS ARE GIVING A PARTY IN HONOR OF AUNT AND UNCLE! ISN'T IT MARVELOUS?
YEH, IT'S PRACTICALLY STUPEFYING!
HMM! EVIDENTLY A DUD, EH?
ALL THAT FRANTIC FUROR WAS JUST OVER AN INVITE TO THE VAN SWANK'S!
YES, THAT'S WOMEN! MY WIFE'S THE SAME WAY ABOUT THE McGINTY'S CLAMBAKE! WELL, GOOD LUCK, MICKEY!
THANKS, MR. O'HARA! I'LL KEEP IN TOUCH WITH YOU!

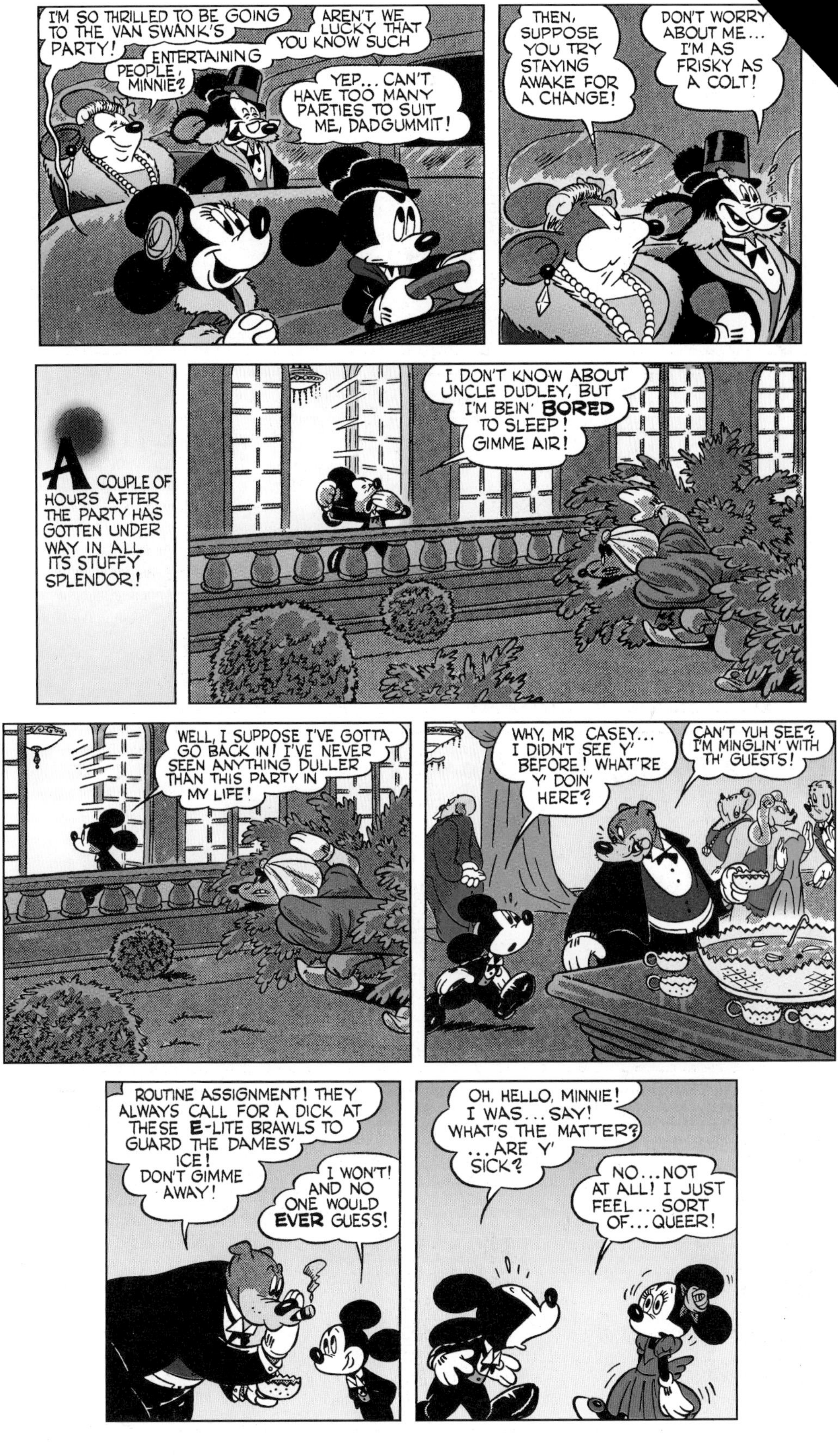
I'M SO THRILLED TO BE GOING TO THE VAN SWANK'S PARTY!
AREN'T WE LUCKY THAT YOU KNOW SUCH ENTERTAINING PEOPLE, MINNIE?
YEP... CAN'T HAVE TOO MANY PARTIES TO SUIT ME, DADGUMMIT!
THEN, SUPPOSE YOU TRY STAYING AWAKE FOR A CHANGE!
DON'T WORRY ABOUT ME... I'M AS FRISKY AS A COLT!
A COUPLE OF HOURS AFTER THE PARTY HAS GOTTEN UNDER WAY IN ALL ITS STUFFY SPLENDOR!
I DON'T KNOW ABOUT UNCLE DUDLEY, BUT I'M BEIN' BORED TO SLEEP! GIMME AIR!
WELL, I SUPPOSE I'VE GOTTA GO BACK IN! I'VE NEVER SEEN ANYTHING DULLER THAN THIS PARTY IN MY LIFE!
WHY, MR CASEY... I DIDN'T SEE Y' BEFORE! WHAT'RE Y' DOIN' HERE?
CAN'T YUH SEE? I'M MINGLIN' WITH TH' GUESTS!
ROUTINE ASSIGNMENT! THEY ALWAYS CALL FOR A DICK AT THESE E-LITE BRAWLS TO GUARD THE DAMES' ICE!
DON'T GIMME AWAY!
I WON'T! AND NO ONE WOULD EVER GUESS!
OH, HELLO, MINNIE! I WAS... SAY! WHAT'S THE MATTER? ... ARE Y' SICK?
NO... NOT AT ALL! I JUST FEEL... SORT OF... QUEER!

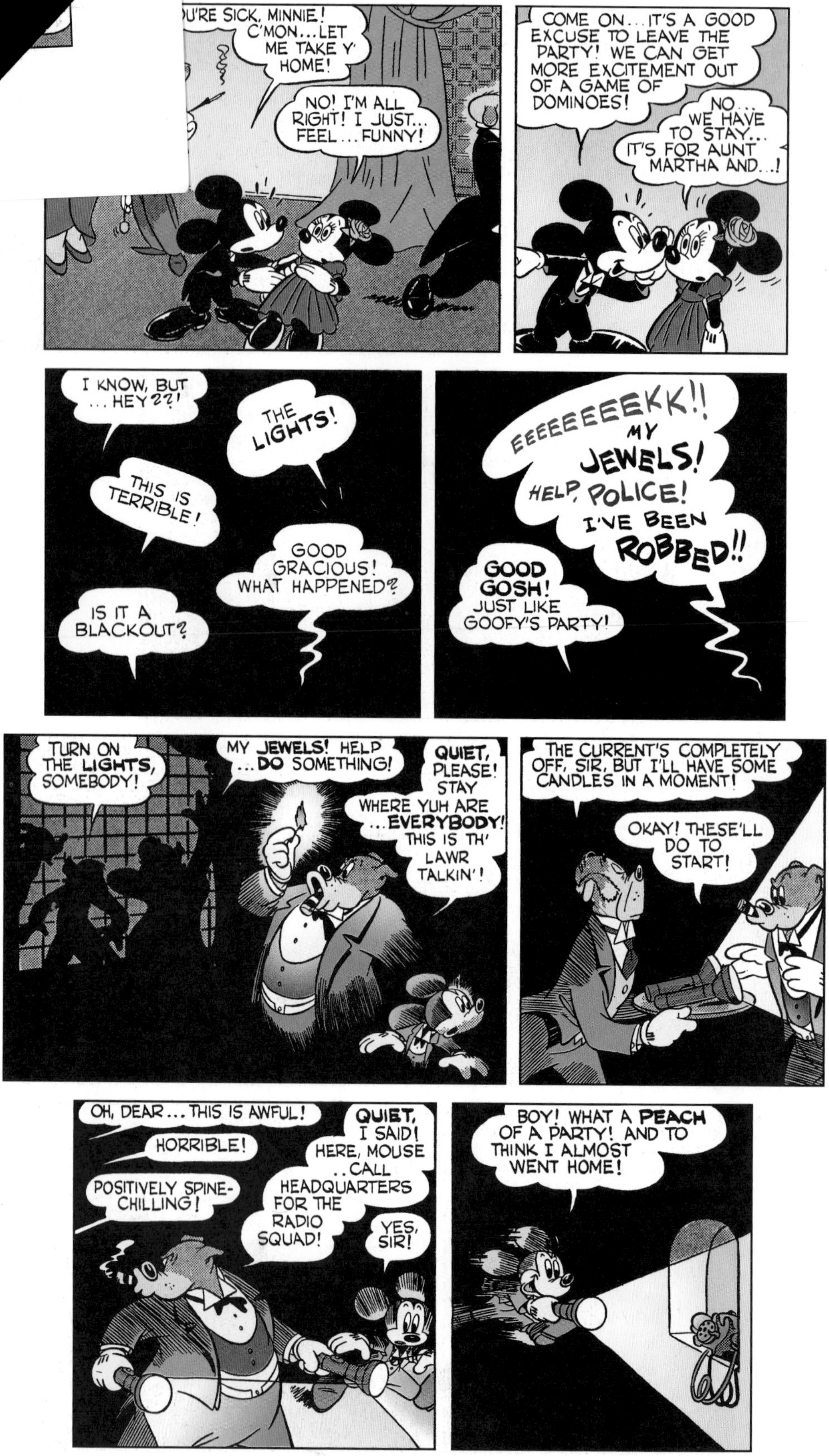
SICK, MINNIE! C'MON...LET ME TAKE Y' HOME!
NO! I'M ALL RIGHT! I JUST... FEEL...FUNNY!
COME ON...IT'S A GOOD EXCUSE TO LEAVE THE PARTY! WE CAN GET MORE EXCITEMENT OUT OF A GAME OF DOMINOES!
NO... WE HAVE TO STAY... IT'S FOR AUNT MARTHA AND...!
I KNOW, BUT ...HEY??!
THE LIGHTS!
THIS IS TERRIBLE!
GOOD GRACIOUS! WHAT HAPPENED?
IS IT A BLACKOUT?
EEEEEEEEKK!! MY JEWELS! HELP, POLICE! I'VE BEEN ROBBED!!
GOOD GOSH! JUST LIKE GOOFY'S PARTY!
TURN ON THE LIGHTS, SOMEBODY!
MY JEWELS! HELP ...DO SOMETHING!
QUIET, PLEASE! STAY WHERE YUH ARE ...EVERYBODY! THIS IS TH' LAWR TALKIN'!
THE CURRENT'S COMPLETELY OFF, SIR, BUT I'LL HAVE SOME CANDLES IN A MOMENT!
OKAY! THESE'LL DO TO START!
OH, DEAR...THIS IS AWFUL!
HORRIBLE!
POSITIVELY SPINE-CHILLING!
QUIET, I SAID! HERE, MOUSE ..CALL HEADQUARTERS FOR THE RADIO SQUAD!
YES, SIR!
BOY! WHAT A PEACH OF A PARTY! AND TO THINK I ALMOST WENT HOME!

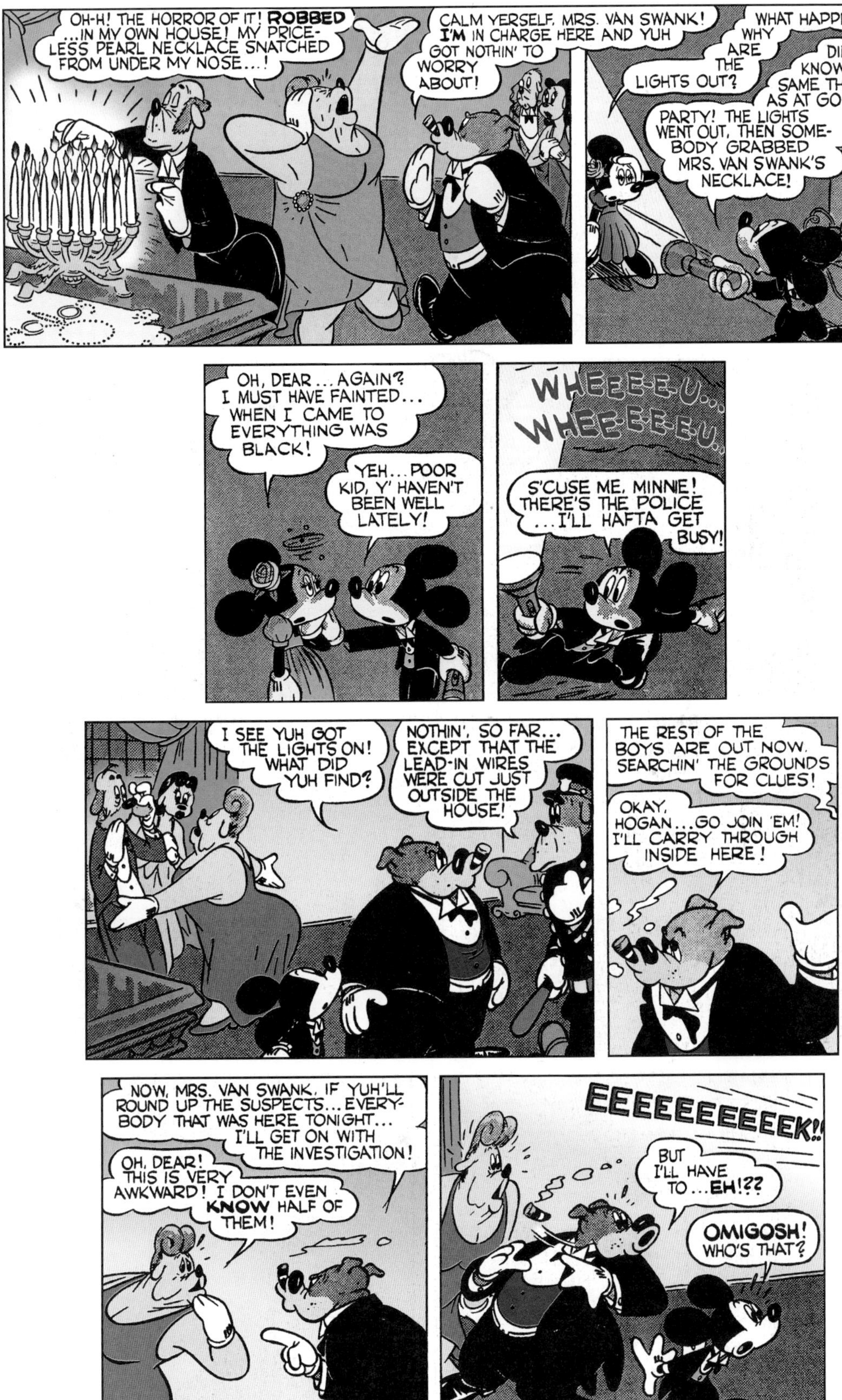

OH-H! THE HORROR OF IT! **ROBBED** ...IN MY OWN HOUSE! MY PRICE-LESS PEARL NECKLACE SNATCHED FROM UNDER MY NOSE...!
CALM YERSELF, MRS. VAN SWANK! **I'M** IN CHARGE HERE AND YUH GOT NOTHIN' TO WORRY ABOUT!
WHAT HAPPENED? WHY ARE THE LIGHTS OUT?
DIDN'T Y' KNOW? THE SAME THING AS AT GOOFY'S PARTY! THE LIGHTS WENT OUT, THEN SOME-BODY GRABBED MRS. VAN SWANK'S NECKLACE!
OH, DEAR... AGAIN? I MUST HAVE FAINTED... WHEN I CAME TO EVERYTHING WAS BLACK!
YEH... POOR KID, Y' HAVEN'T BEEN WELL LATELY!
WHEEE-E-U... WHEE-E-E-E-U...
S'CUSE ME, MINNIE! THERE'S THE POLICE ...I'LL HAFTA GET BUSY!
I SEE YUH GOT THE LIGHTS ON! WHAT DID YUH FIND?
NOTHIN', SO FAR... EXCEPT THAT THE LEAD-IN WIRES WERE CUT JUST OUTSIDE THE HOUSE!
THE REST OF THE BOYS ARE OUT NOW, SEARCHIN' THE GROUNDS FOR CLUES!
OKAY, HOGAN... GO JOIN 'EM! I'LL CARRY THROUGH INSIDE HERE!
NOW, MRS. VAN SWANK, IF YUH'LL ROUND UP THE SUSPECTS... EVERY-BODY THAT WAS HERE TONIGHT... I'LL GET ON WITH THE INVESTIGATION!
OH, DEAR! THIS IS VERY AWKWARD! I DON'T EVEN **KNOW** HALF OF THEM!
EEEEEEEEEEK!!
BUT I'LL HAVE TO... **EH**!??
OMIGOSH! WHO'S THAT?

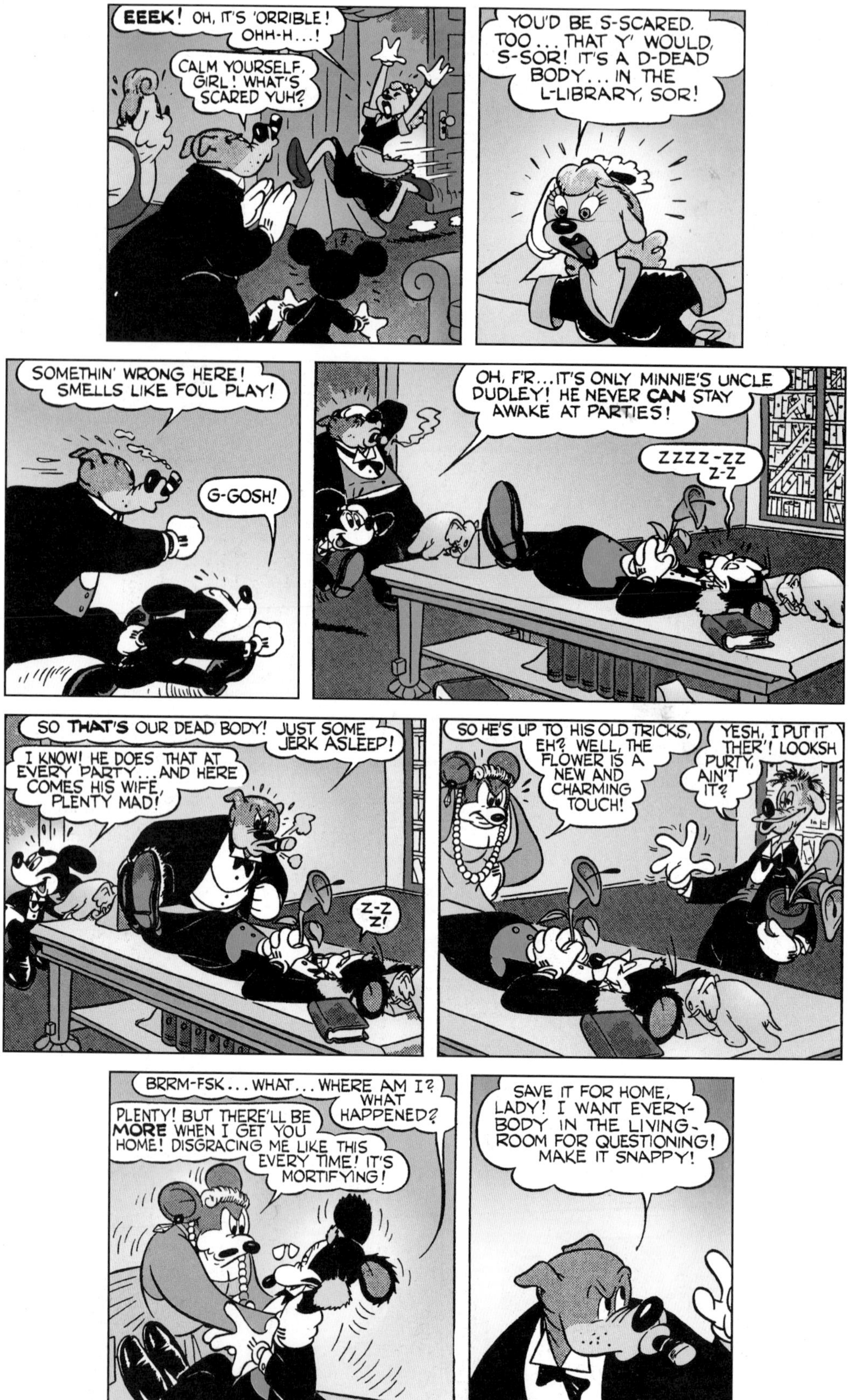
EEEK! OH, IT'S 'ORRIBLE! OHH-H...!
CALM YOURSELF, GIRL! WHAT'S SCARED YUH?
YOU'D BE S-SCARED, TOO... THAT Y' WOULD, S-SOR! IT'S A D-DEAD BODY... IN THE L-LIBRARY, SOR!
SOMETHIN' WRONG HERE! SMELLS LIKE FOUL PLAY!
G-GOSH!
OH, F'R... IT'S ONLY MINNIE'S UNCLE DUDLEY! HE NEVER CAN STAY AWAKE AT PARTIES!
ZZZZ-ZZ Z-Z
SO THAT'S OUR DEAD BODY! JUST SOME JERK ASLEEP!
I KNOW! HE DOES THAT AT EVERY PARTY... AND HERE COMES HIS WIFE, PLENTY MAD!
Z-Z Z!
SO HE'S UP TO HIS OLD TRICKS, EH? WELL, THE FLOWER IS A NEW AND CHARMING TOUCH!
YESH, I PUT IT THER'! LOOKSH PURTY, AIN'T IT?
BRRM-FSK... WHAT... WHERE AM I? WHAT HAPPENED?
PLENTY! BUT THERE'LL BE MORE WHEN I GET YOU HOME! DISGRACING ME LIKE THIS EVERY TIME! IT'S MORTIFYING!
SAVE IT FOR HOME, LADY! I WANT EVERY-BODY IN THE LIVING-ROOM FOR QUESTIONING! MAKE IT SNAPPY!

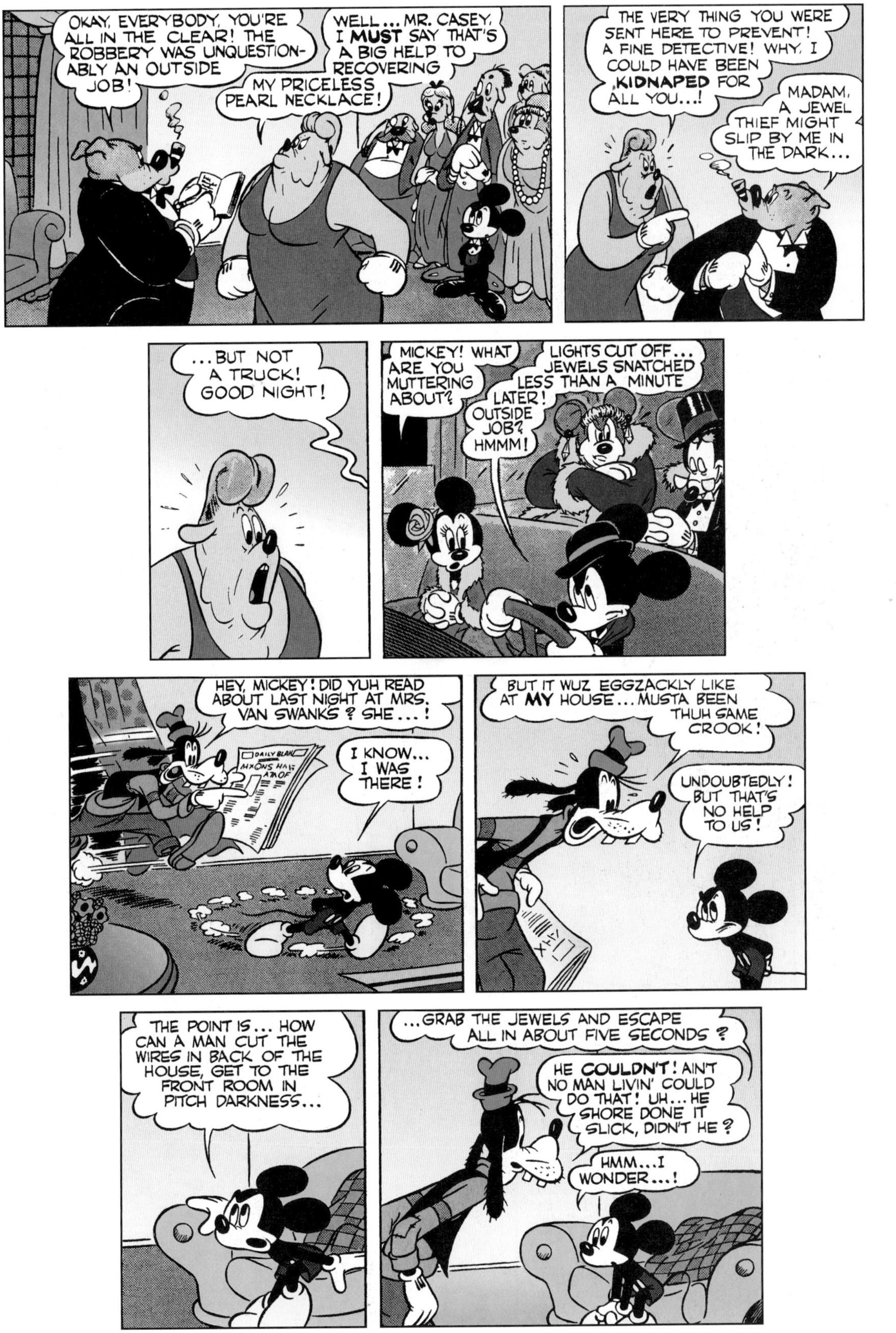
OKAY, EVERYBODY, YOU'RE ALL IN THE CLEAR! THE ROBBERY WAS UNQUESTIONABLY AN OUTSIDE JOB!
WELL... MR. CASEY, I MUST SAY THAT'S A BIG HELP TO RECOVERING
MY PRICELESS PEARL NECKLACE!
THE VERY THING YOU WERE SENT HERE TO PREVENT! A FINE DETECTIVE! WHY, I COULD HAVE BEEN KIDNAPED FOR ALL YOU...!
MADAM, A JEWEL THIEF MIGHT SLIP BY ME IN THE DARK...
...BUT NOT A TRUCK! GOOD NIGHT!
MICKEY! WHAT ARE YOU MUTTERING ABOUT?
LIGHTS CUT OFF... JEWELS SNATCHED LESS THAN A MINUTE LATER! OUTSIDE JOB? HMMM!
HEY, MICKEY! DID YUH READ ABOUT LAST NIGHT AT MRS. VAN SWANKS? SHE...!
DAILY BLAH
I KNOW... I WAS THERE!
BUT IT WUZ EGGZACKLY LIKE AT MY HOUSE... MUSTA BEEN THUH SAME CROOK!
UNDOUBTEDLY! BUT THAT'S NO HELP TO US!
THE POINT IS... HOW CAN A MAN CUT THE WIRES IN BACK OF THE HOUSE, GET TO THE FRONT ROOM IN PITCH DARKNESS...
...GRAB THE JEWELS AND ESCAPE ALL IN ABOUT FIVE SECONDS?
HE COULDN'T! AIN'T NO MAN LIVIN' COULD DO THAT! UH... HE SHORE DONE IT SLICK, DIDN'T HE?
HMM... I WONDER...!

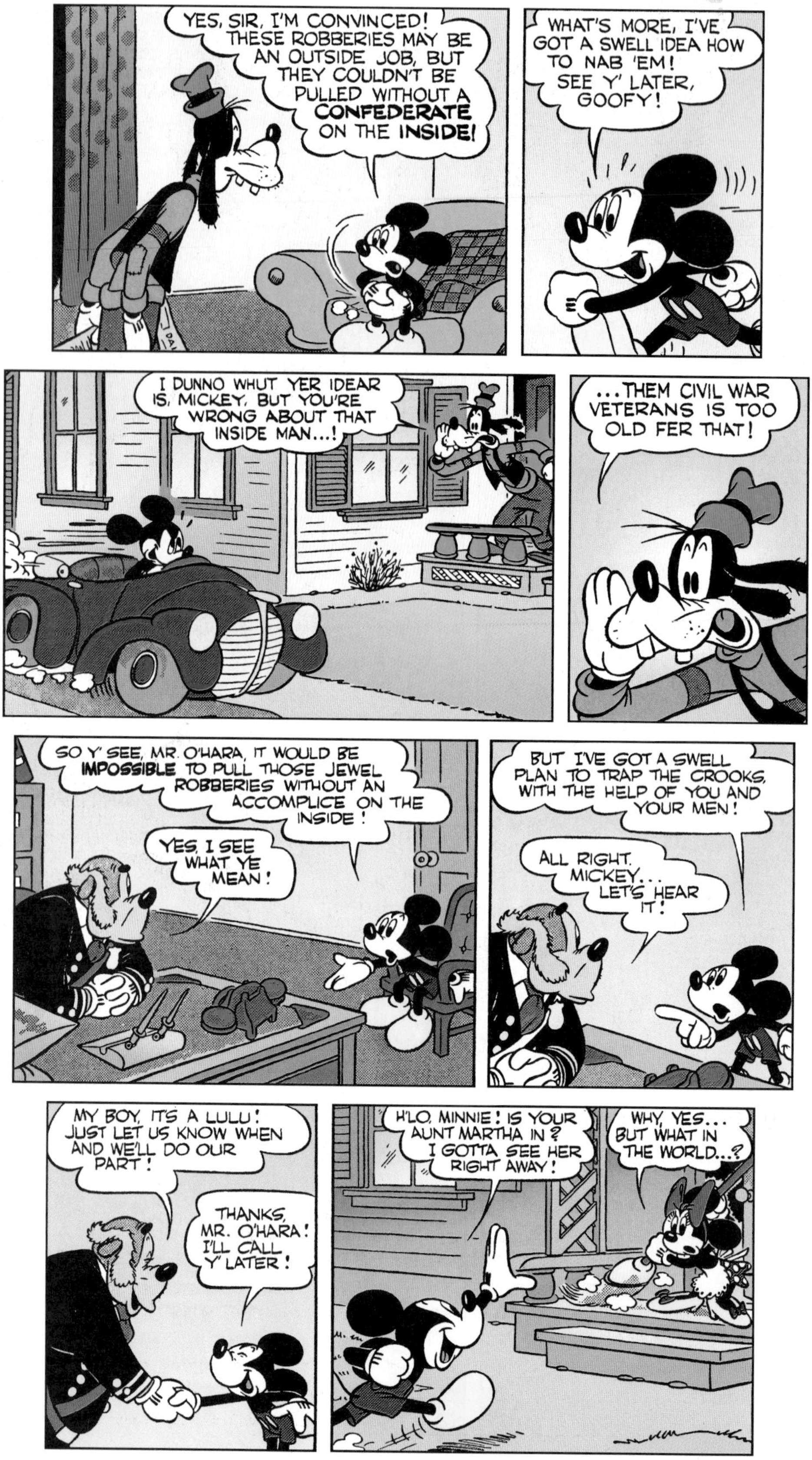
YES, SIR, I'M CONVINCED! THESE ROBBERIES MAY BE AN OUTSIDE JOB, BUT THEY COULDN'T BE PULLED WITHOUT A CONFEDERATE ON THE INSIDE!
WHAT'S MORE, I'VE GOT A SWELL IDEA HOW TO NAB 'EM! SEE Y' LATER, GOOFY!
I DUNNO WHUT YER IDEAR IS, MICKEY, BUT YOU'RE WRONG ABOUT THAT INSIDE MAN...!
...THEM CIVIL WAR VETERANS IS TOO OLD FER THAT!
SO Y' SEE, MR. O'HARA, IT WOULD BE IMPOSSIBLE TO PULL THOSE JEWEL ROBBERIES WITHOUT AN ACCOMPLICE ON THE INSIDE!
YES, I SEE WHAT YE MEAN!
BUT I'VE GOT A SWELL PLAN TO TRAP THE CROOKS, WITH THE HELP OF YOU AND YOUR MEN!
ALL RIGHT, MICKEY... LET'S HEAR IT!
MY BOY, IT'S A LULU! JUST LET US KNOW WHEN AND WE'LL DO OUR PART!
THANKS, MR. O'HARA! I'LL CALL Y' LATER!
H'LO, MINNIE! IS YOUR AUNT MARTHA IN? I GOTTA SEE HER RIGHT AWAY!
WHY, YES... BUT WHAT IN THE WORLD...?

TO BE CONTINUED!

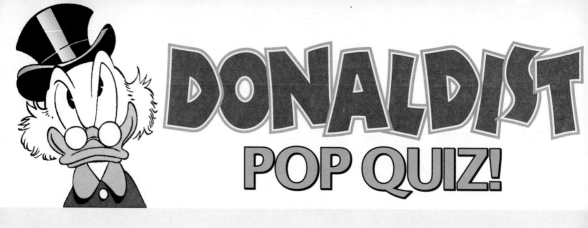

DONALDIST POP QUIZ!

don • ald • ism \ dän'-ld-iz'-em \ *n* : the research of Disney comics, and/or the fan culture that is found among Disney comics aficionados (Jon Gisle, 1973)

1. Who is Scrooge McDuck's "old flame" from the Yukon?

2. Who *wants* to be "Scroogie's" *new* love interest?

3. And how will Scrooge be celebrating his birthday this year? (Hint: *Not* by going out on a date!)

You can find the answers at the bottom of this page, but you'll have more fun finding them in Gemstone's 160-page anniversary book:

UNCLE SCROOGE: A LITTLE SOMETHING SPECIAL!

- *Discover Carl Barks' "Seven Cities of Cibola," Scrooge's richest treasure hunt!*

- *Watch Scrooge earn his Number One Dime in Tony Strobl's "Getting That Healthy Wealthy Feeling" — uncut for the first time in North America!*

- *Thrilling tightwad tales by Marco Rota ("The Money Ocean"), William Van Horn ("Windfall on Mt. G'zoontight"), and Romano Scarpa (the never-before-reprinted "Witness Persecution")!*

- *Don Rosa's feature-length anniversary epic "A Little Something Special"... what else could this book be named after?*

GEMSTONE PUBLISHING
presents
**WALT DISNEY TREASURES
VOLUME TWO**
On Sale Now!

(ANSWERS: 1. Glittering Goldie;
2. Brigitta MacBridge; 3. Enjoying his copy
of *Walt Disney Treasures, Volume 2*)

www.gemstonepub.com/disney

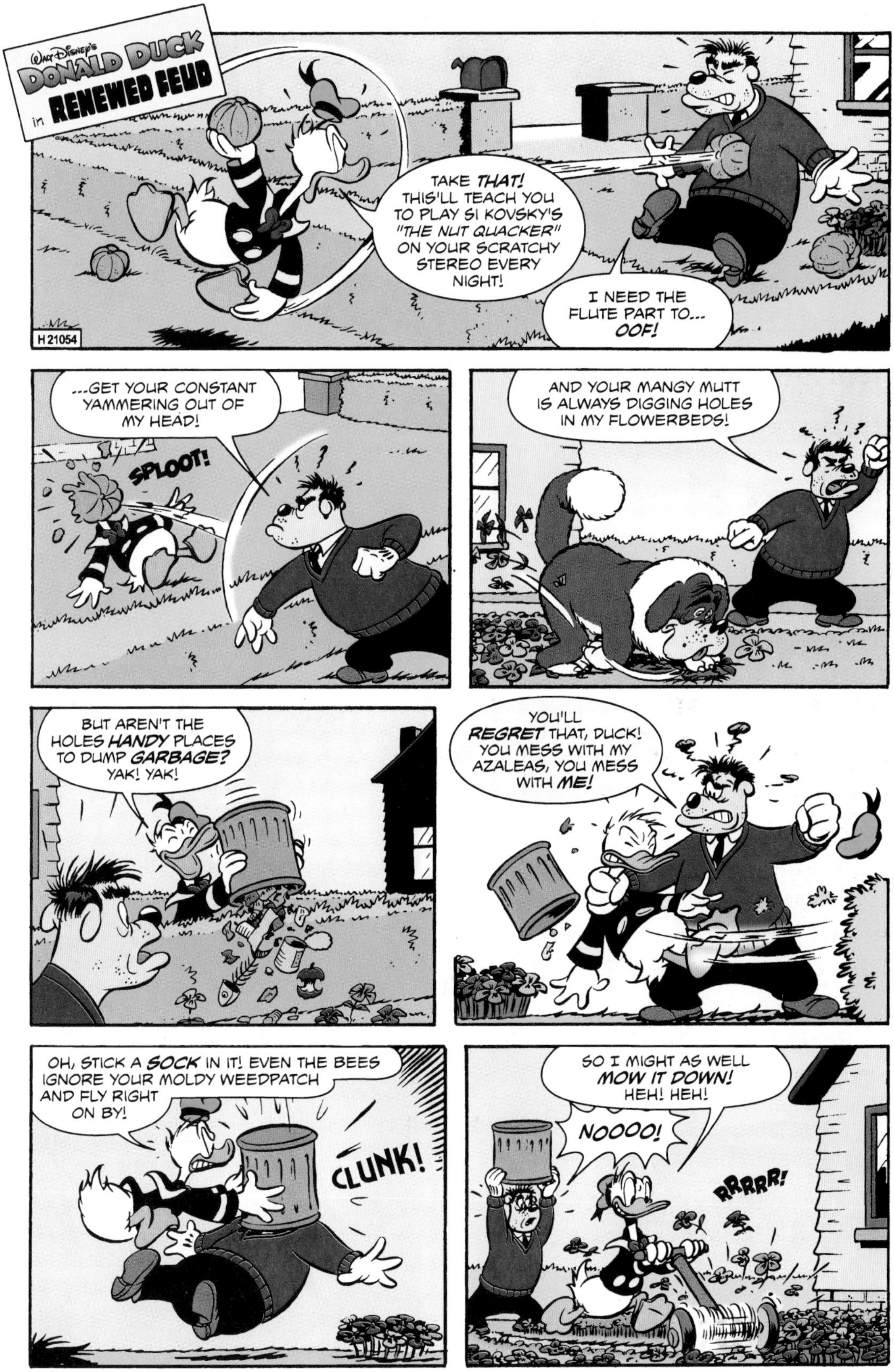
WALT DISNEY'S DONALD DUCK in RENEWED FEUD
TAKE THAT! THIS'LL TEACH YOU TO PLAY SI KOVSKY'S "THE NUT QUACKER" ON YOUR SCRATCHY STEREO EVERY NIGHT!
I NEED THE FLUTE PART TO... OOF!
H 21054
...GET YOUR CONSTANT YAMMERING OUT OF MY HEAD!
SPLOOT!
AND YOUR MANGY MUTT IS ALWAYS DIGGING HOLES IN MY FLOWERBEDS!
BUT AREN'T THE HOLES HANDY PLACES TO DUMP GARBAGE? YAK! YAK!
YOU'LL REGRET THAT, DUCK! YOU MESS WITH MY AZALEAS, YOU MESS WITH ME!
OH, STICK A SOCK IN IT! EVEN THE BEES IGNORE YOUR MOLDY WEEDPATCH AND FLY RIGHT ON BY!
CLUNK!
SO I MIGHT AS WELL MOW IT DOWN! HEH! HEH!
NOOOO!
RRRRR!

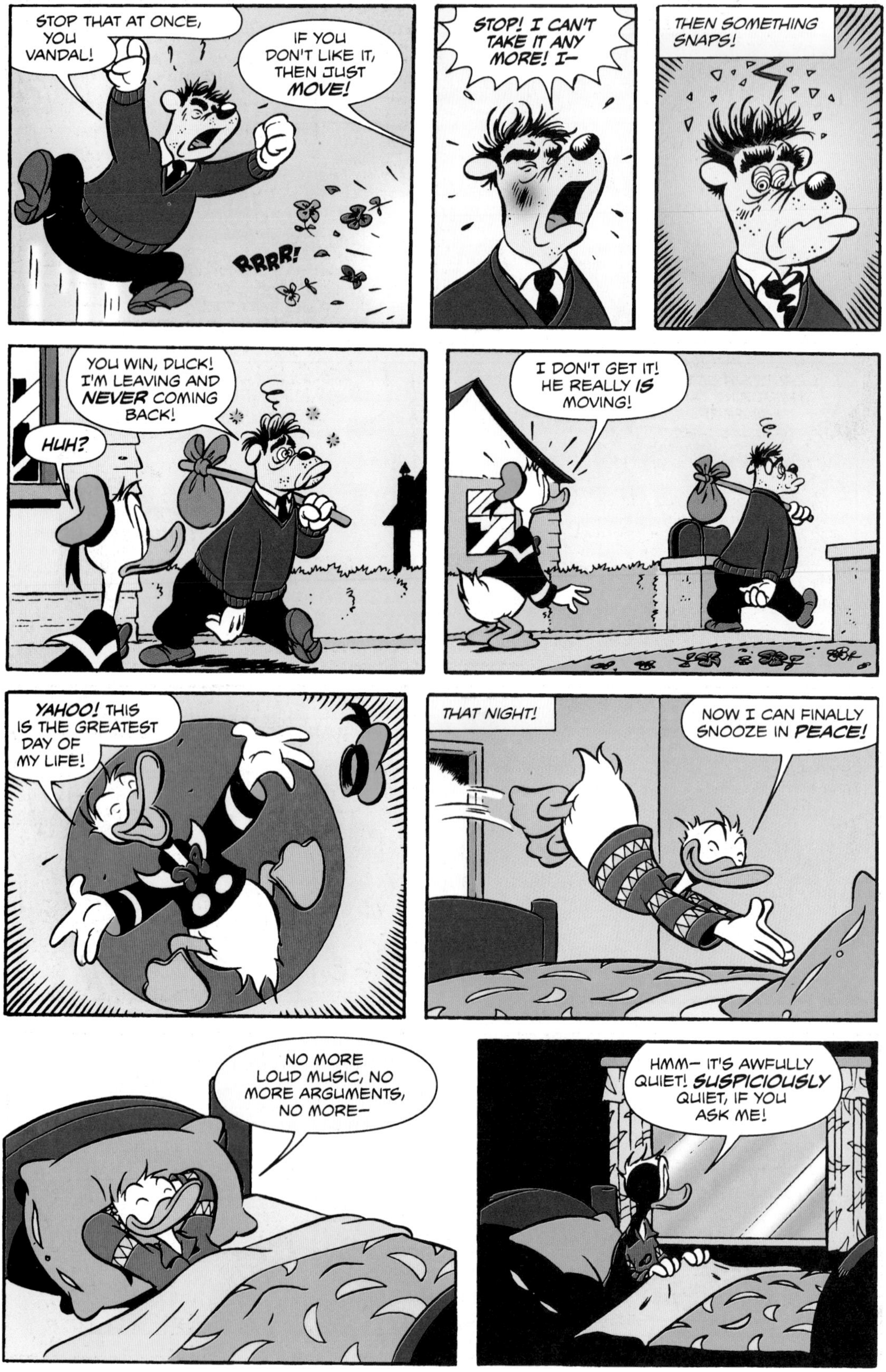
STOP THAT AT ONCE, YOU VANDAL!
IF YOU DON'T LIKE IT, THEN JUST MOVE!
RRRR!
STOP! I CAN'T TAKE IT ANY MORE! I—
THEN SOMETHING SNAPS!
YOU WIN, DUCK! I'M LEAVING AND NEVER COMING BACK!
HUH?
I DON'T GET IT! HE REALLY IS MOVING!
YAHOO! THIS IS THE GREATEST DAY OF MY LIFE!
THAT NIGHT!
NOW I CAN FINALLY SNOOZE IN PEACE!
NO MORE LOUD MUSIC, NO MORE ARGUMENTS, NO MORE—
HMM— IT'S AWFULLY QUIET! SUSPICIOUSLY QUIET, IF YOU ASK ME!

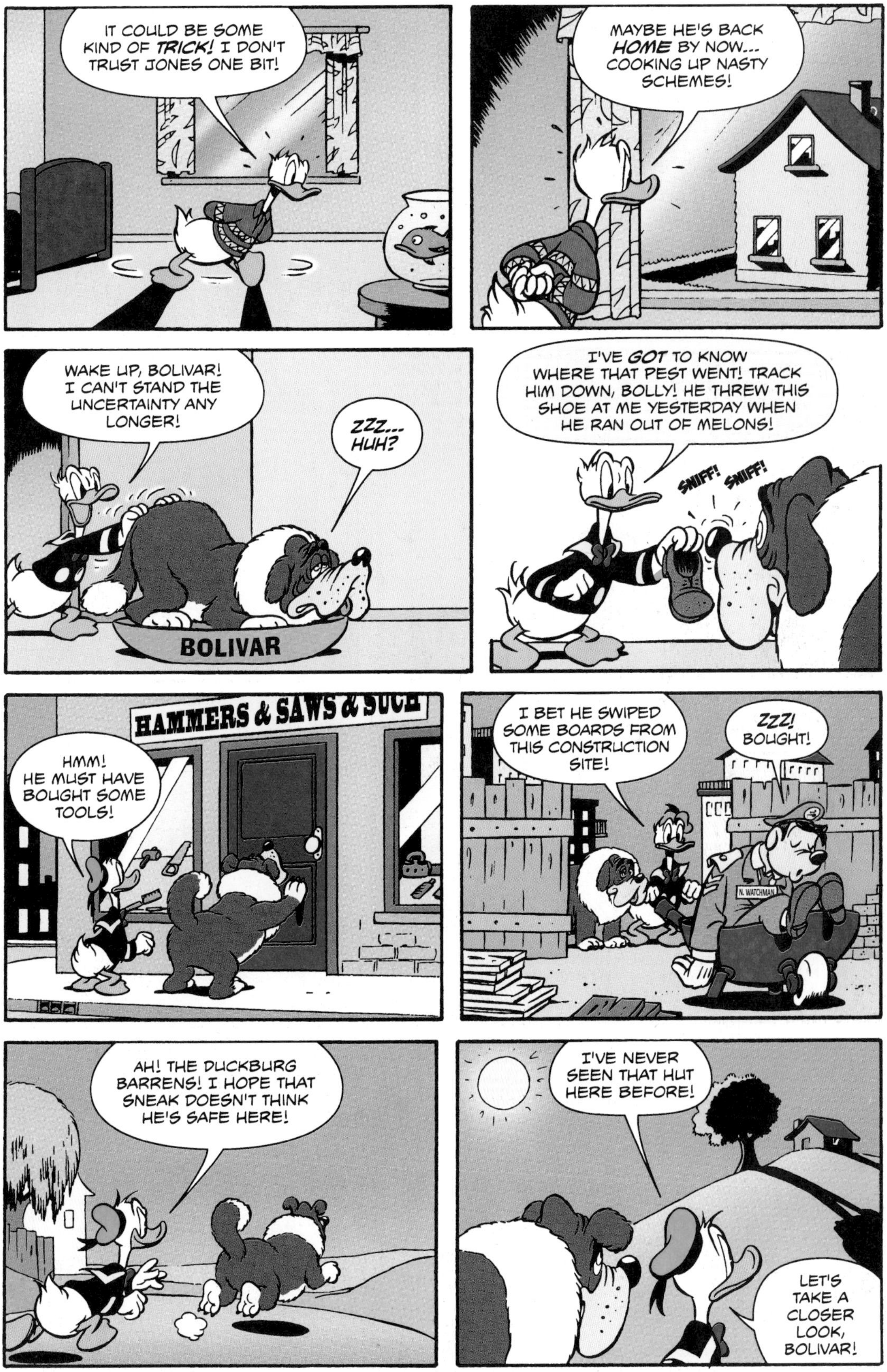

IT COULD BE SOME KIND OF TRICK! I DON'T TRUST JONES ONE BIT!
MAYBE HE'S BACK HOME BY NOW... COOKING UP NASTY SCHEMES!
WAKE UP, BOLIVAR! I CAN'T STAND THE UNCERTAINTY ANY LONGER!
ZZZ... HUH?
BOLIVAR
I'VE GOT TO KNOW WHERE THAT PEST WENT! TRACK HIM DOWN, BOLLY! HE THREW THIS SHOE AT ME YESTERDAY WHEN HE RAN OUT OF MELONS!
SNIFF! SNIFF!
HAMMERS & SAWS & SUCH
HMM! HE MUST HAVE BOUGHT SOME TOOLS!
I BET HE SWIPED SOME BOARDS FROM THIS CONSTRUCTION SITE!
ZZZ! BOUGHT!
N. WATCHMAN
AH! THE DUCKBURG BARRENS! I HOPE THAT SNEAK DOESN'T THINK HE'S SAFE HERE!
I'VE NEVER SEEN THAT HUT HERE BEFORE!
LET'S TAKE A CLOSER LOOK, BOLIVAR!

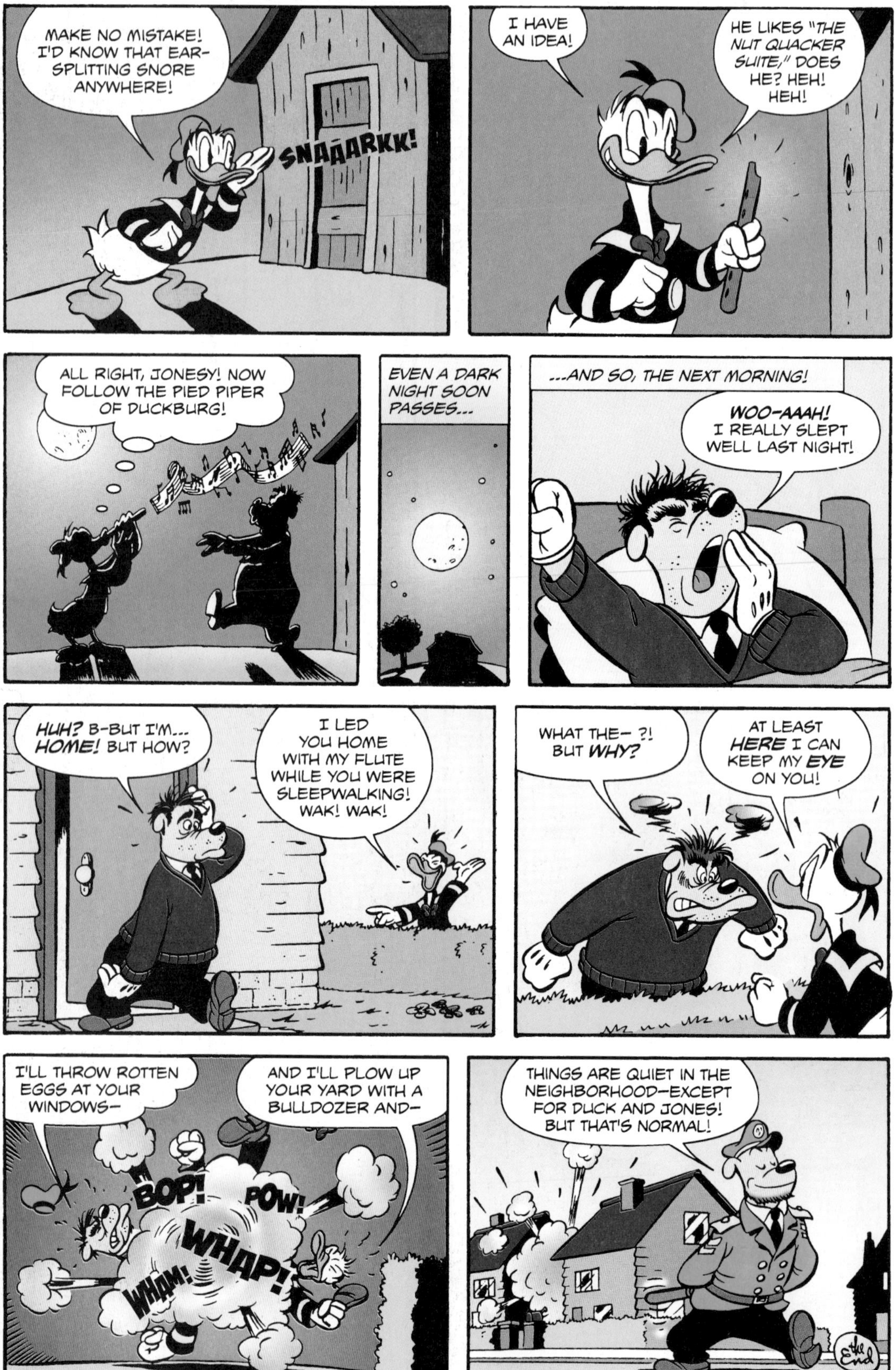
MAKE NO MISTAKE! I'D KNOW THAT EAR-SPLITTING SNORE ANYWHERE!
SNAAARKK!
I HAVE AN IDEA!
HE LIKES "THE NUT QUACKER SUITE," DOES HE? HEH! HEH!
ALL RIGHT, JONESY! NOW FOLLOW THE PIED PIPER OF DUCKBURG!
EVEN A DARK NIGHT SOON PASSES...
...AND SO, THE NEXT MORNING!
WOO-AAAH! I REALLY SLEPT WELL LAST NIGHT!
HUH? B-BUT I'M... HOME! BUT HOW?
I LED YOU HOME WITH MY FLUTE WHILE YOU WERE SLEEPWALKING! WAK! WAK!
WHAT THE- ?! BUT WHY?
AT LEAST HERE I CAN KEEP MY EYE ON YOU!
I'LL THROW ROTTEN EGGS AT YOUR WINDOWS-
AND I'LL PLOW UP YOUR YARD WITH A BULLDOZER AND-
BOP!
POW!
WHAP!
WHAM!
THINGS ARE QUIET IN THE NEIGHBORHOOD—EXCEPT FOR DUCK AND JONES! BUT THAT'S NORMAL!
the End

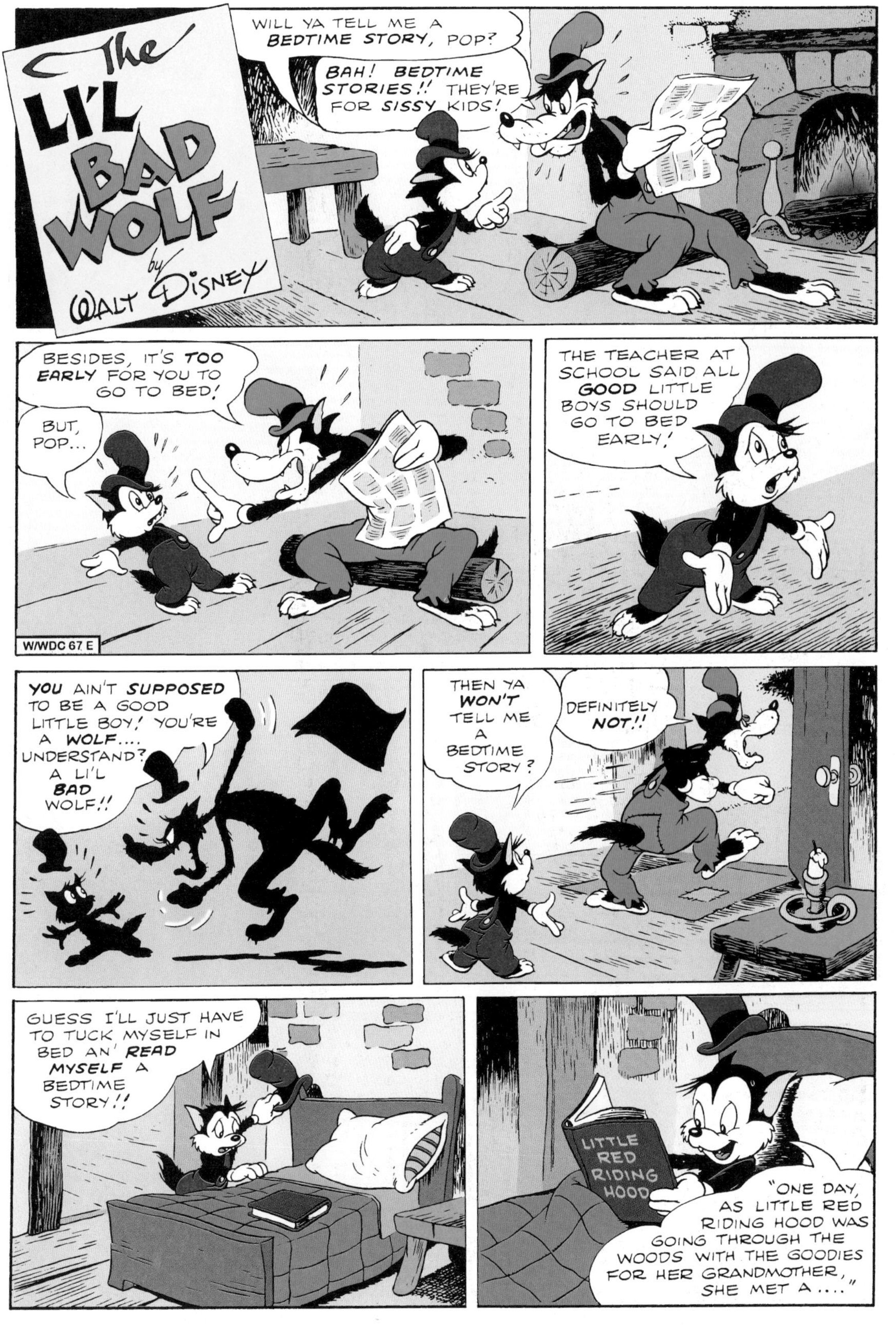
The LI'L BAD WOLF
by WALT DISNEY
WILL YA TELL ME A BEDTIME STORY, POP?
BAH! BEDTIME STORIES!! THEY'RE FOR SISSY KIDS!
BESIDES, IT'S TOO EARLY FOR YOU TO GO TO BED!
BUT, POP...
W/WDC 67 E
THE TEACHER AT SCHOOL SAID ALL GOOD LITTLE BOYS SHOULD GO TO BED EARLY!
YOU AIN'T SUPPOSED TO BE A GOOD LITTLE BOY! YOU'RE A WOLF.... UNDERSTAND? A LI'L BAD WOLF!!
THEN YA WON'T TELL ME A BEDTIME STORY?
DEFINITELY NOT!!
GUESS I'LL JUST HAVE TO TUCK MYSELF IN BED AN' READ MYSELF A BEDTIME STORY!!
LITTLE RED RIDING HOOD
"ONE DAY, AS LITTLE RED RIDING HOOD WAS GOING THROUGH THE WOODS WITH THE GOODIES FOR HER GRANDMOTHER, SHE MET A ...."

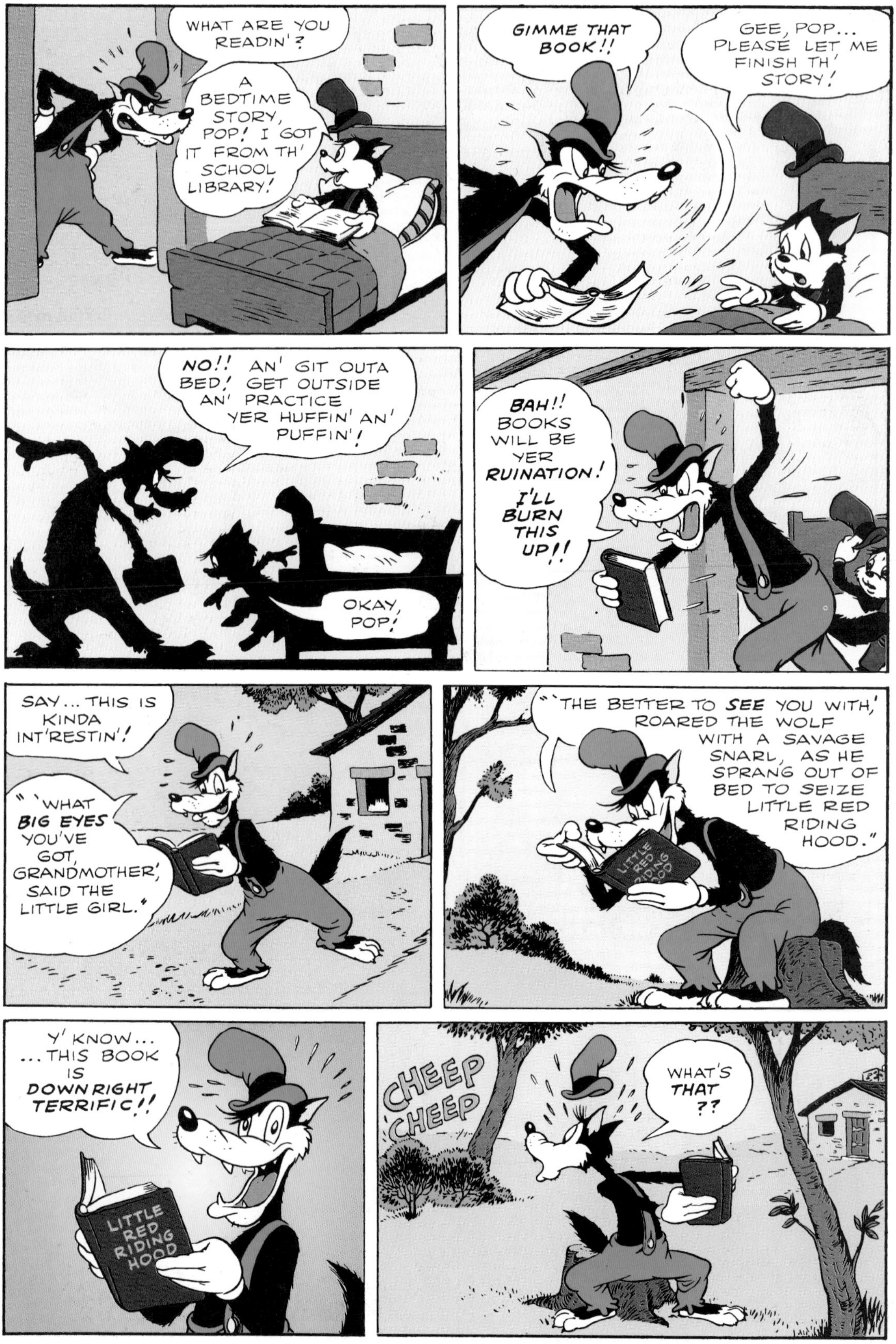
WHAT ARE YOU READIN'?
A BEDTIME STORY, POP! I GOT IT FROM TH' SCHOOL LIBRARY!
GIMME THAT BOOK!!
GEE, POP... PLEASE LET ME FINISH TH' STORY!
NO!! AN' GIT OUTA BED! GET OUTSIDE AN' PRACTICE YER HUFFIN' AN' PUFFIN'!
OKAY, POP!
BAH!! BOOKS WILL BE YER RUINATION! I'LL BURN THIS UP!!
SAY... THIS IS KINDA INT'RESTIN'!
"'WHAT BIG EYES YOU'VE GOT, GRANDMOTHER', SAID THE LITTLE GIRL."
"'THE BETTER TO SEE YOU WITH,' ROARED THE WOLF WITH A SAVAGE SNARL, AS HE SPRANG OUT OF BED TO SEIZE LITTLE RED RIDING HOOD."
LITTLE RED RIDING HOOD
Y' KNOW... ...THIS BOOK IS DOWNRIGHT TERRIFIC!!
LITTLE RED RIDING HOOD
CHEEP CHEEP
WHAT'S THAT??

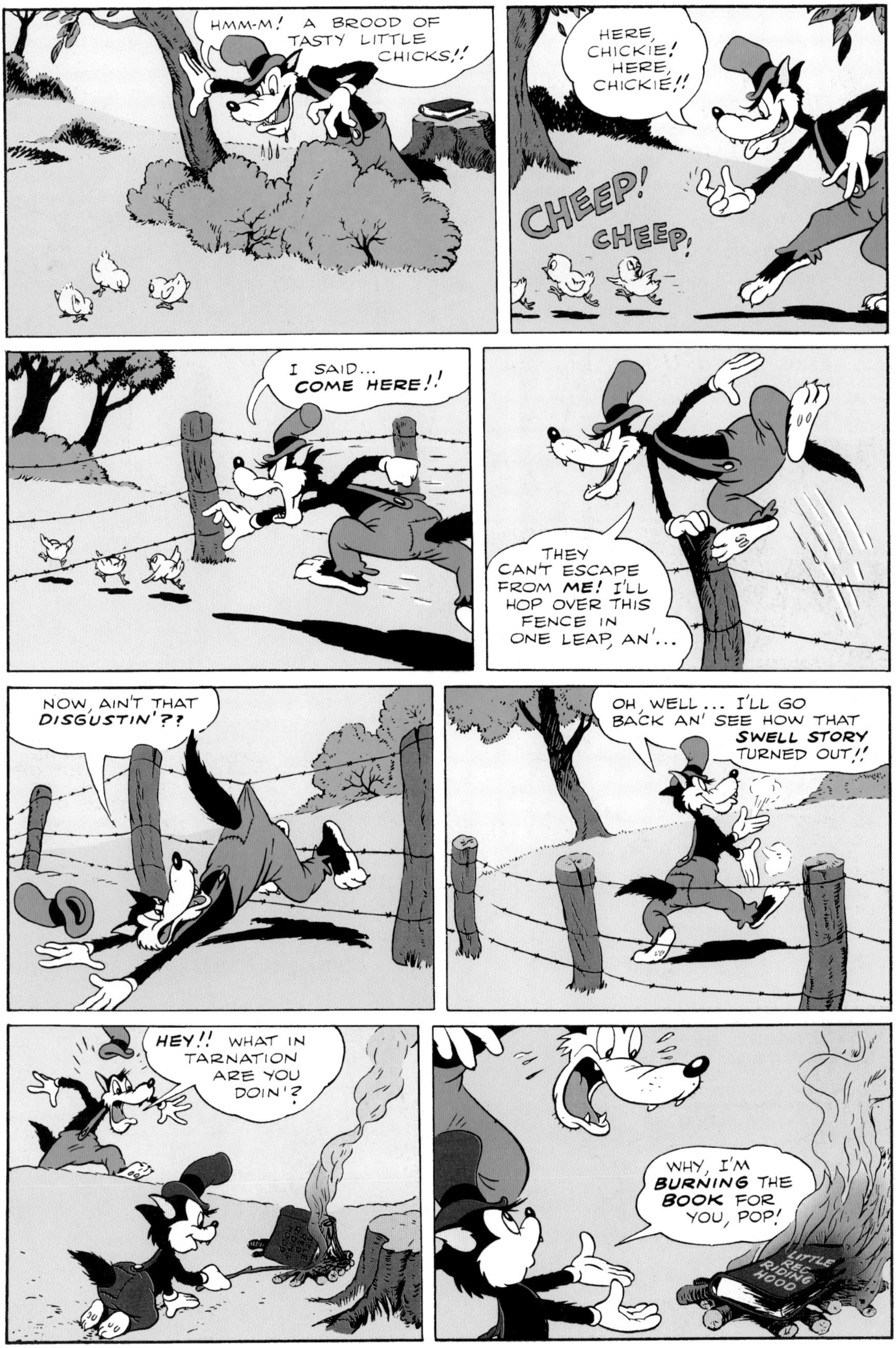

HMM-M! A BROOD OF TASTY LITTLE CHICKS!!
HERE, CHICKIE! HERE, CHICKIE!!
CHEEP! CHEEP!
I SAID... **COME HERE!!**
THEY CAN'T ESCAPE FROM **ME!** I'LL HOP OVER THIS FENCE IN ONE LEAP, AN'...
NOW, AIN'T THAT **DISGUSTIN'??**
OH, WELL... I'LL GO BACK AN' SEE HOW THAT **SWELL STORY** TURNED OUT!!
HEY!! WHAT IN TARNATION ARE YOU DOIN'?
WHY, I'M **BURNING** THE **BOOK** FOR YOU, POP!
LITTLE RED RIDING HOOD

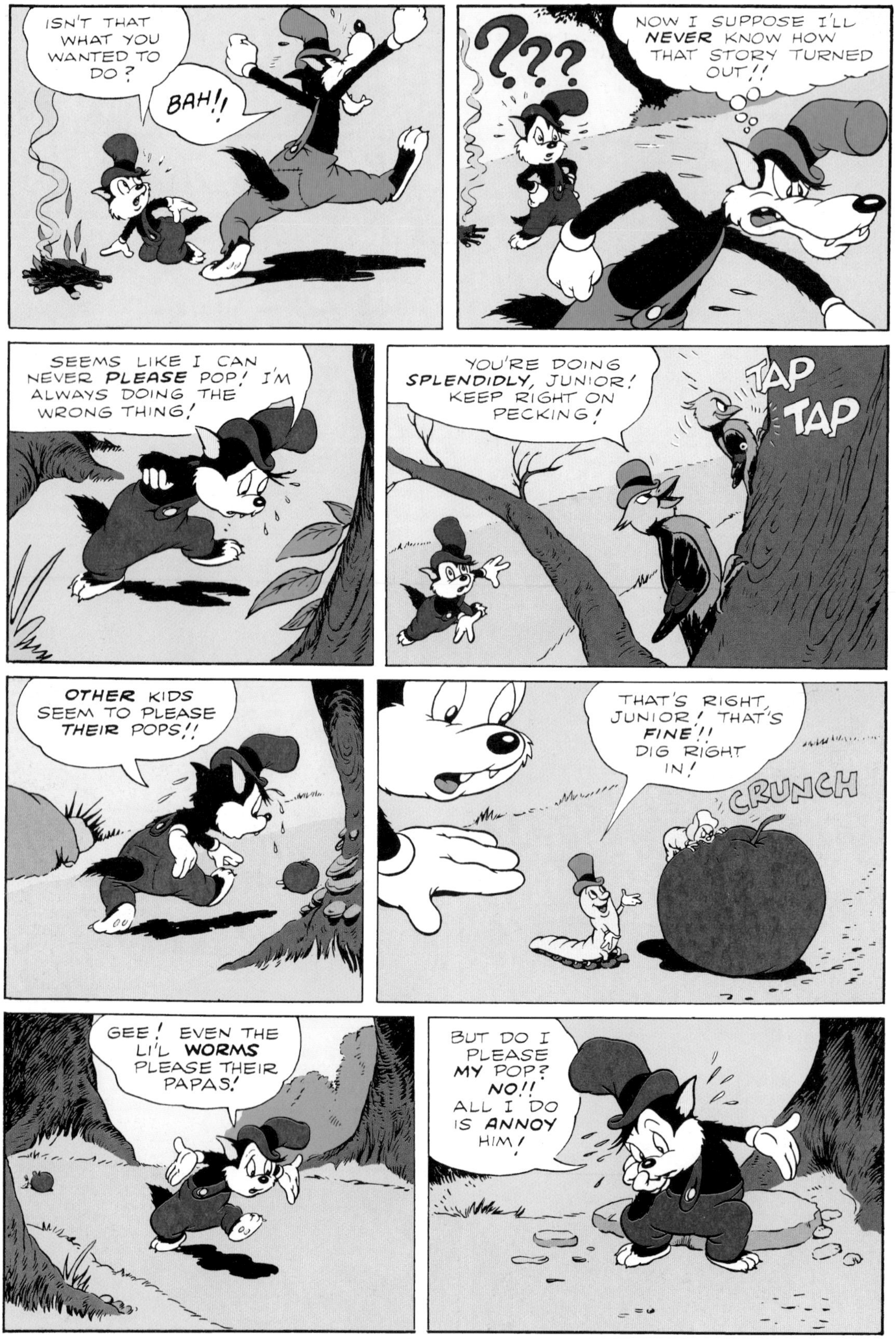
ISN'T THAT WHAT YOU WANTED TO DO?
BAH!!
NOW I SUPPOSE I'LL NEVER KNOW HOW THAT STORY TURNED OUT!!
SEEMS LIKE I CAN NEVER PLEASE POP! I'M ALWAYS DOING THE WRONG THING!
YOU'RE DOING SPLENDIDLY, JUNIOR! KEEP RIGHT ON PECKING!
TAP
TAP
OTHER KIDS SEEM TO PLEASE THEIR POPS!!
THAT'S RIGHT, JUNIOR! THAT'S FINE!! DIG RIGHT IN!
CRUNCH
GEE! EVEN THE LI'L WORMS PLEASE THEIR PAPAS!
BUT DO I PLEASE MY POP? NO!! ALL I DO IS ANNOY HIM!

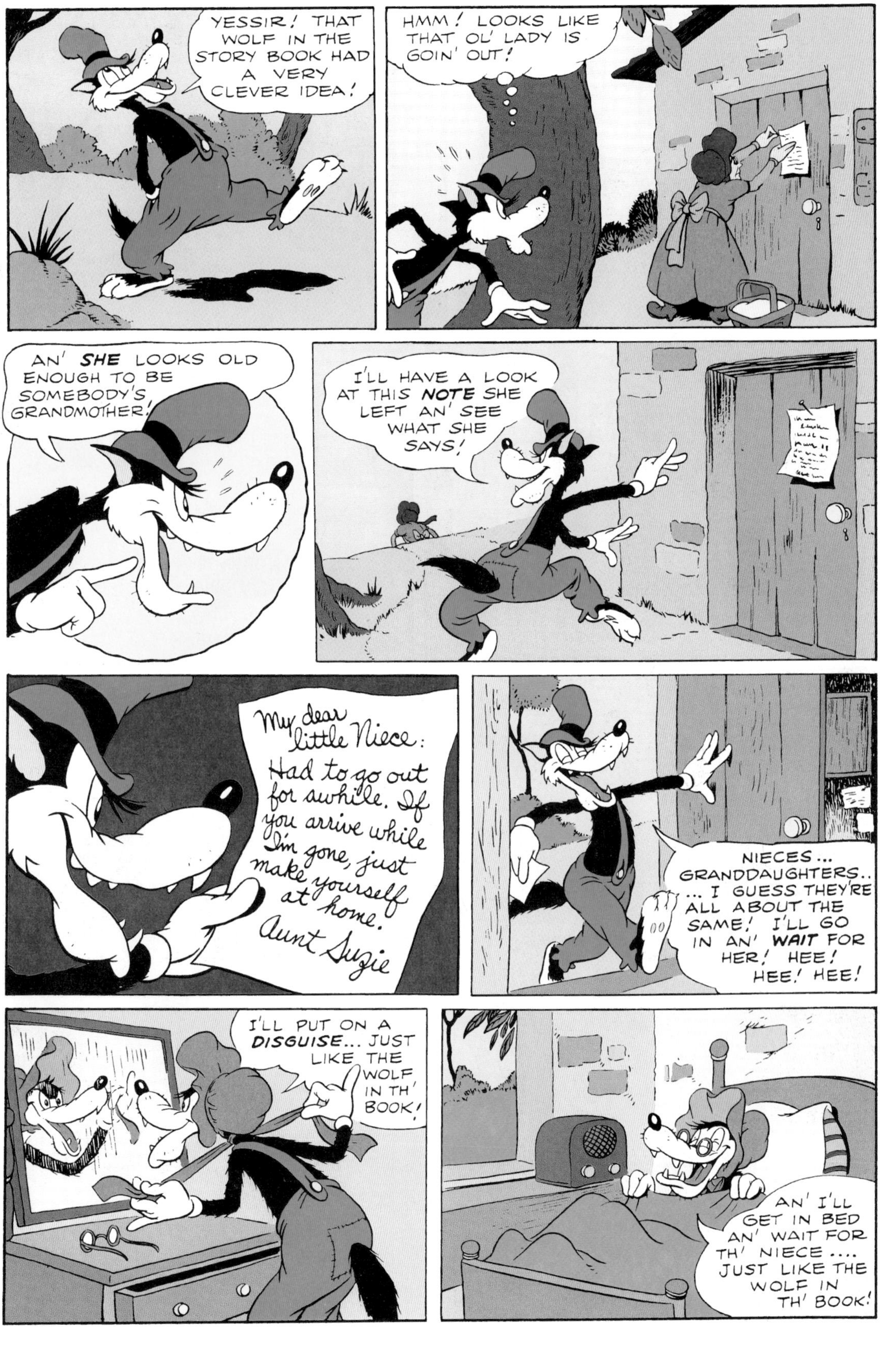
YESSIR! THAT WOLF IN THE STORY BOOK HAD A VERY CLEVER IDEA!
HMM! LOOKS LIKE THAT OL' LADY IS GOIN' OUT!
AN' SHE LOOKS OLD ENOUGH TO BE SOMEBODY'S GRANDMOTHER!
I'LL HAVE A LOOK AT THIS NOTE SHE LEFT AN' SEE WHAT SHE SAYS!
My dear little Niece: Had to go out for awhile. If you arrive while I'm gone, just make yourself at home. Aunt Suzie
NIECES... GRANDDAUGHTERS.. ... I GUESS THEY'RE ALL ABOUT THE SAME! I'LL GO IN AN' WAIT FOR HER! HEE! HEE! HEE!
I'LL PUT ON A DISGUISE... JUST LIKE THE WOLF IN TH' BOOK!
AN' I'LL GET IN BED AN' WAIT FOR TH' NIECE.... JUST LIKE THE WOLF IN TH' BOOK!

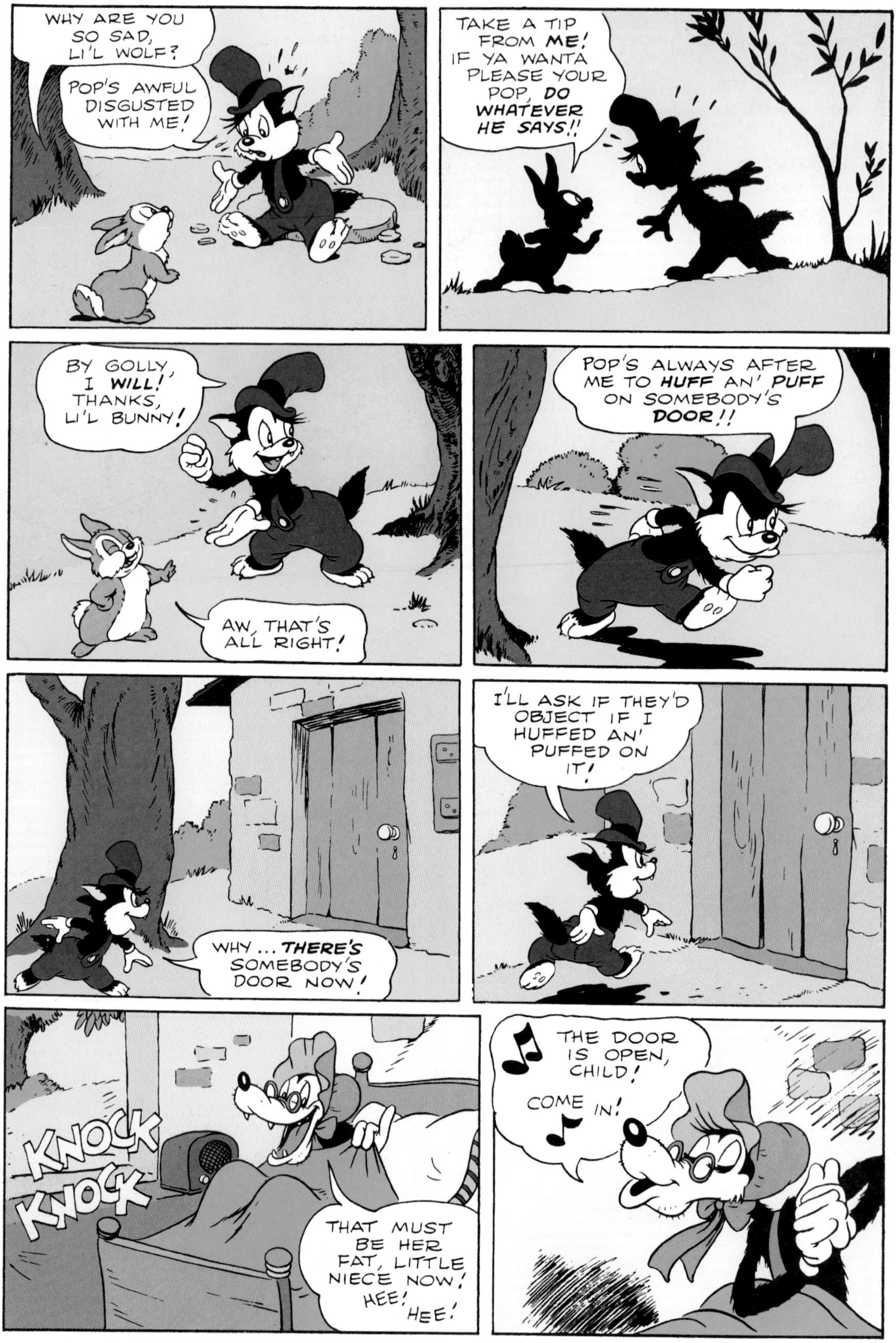
WHY ARE YOU SO SAD, LI'L WOLF?
POP'S AWFUL DISGUSTED WITH ME!
TAKE A TIP FROM ME! IF YA WANTA PLEASE YOUR POP, DO WHATEVER HE SAYS!!
BY GOLLY, I WILL! THANKS, LI'L BUNNY!
AW, THAT'S ALL RIGHT!
POP'S ALWAYS AFTER ME TO HUFF AN' PUFF ON SOMEBODY'S DOOR!!
WHY ... THERE'S SOMEBODY'S DOOR NOW!
I'LL ASK IF THEY'D OBJECT IF I HUFFED AN' PUFFED ON IT!
KNOCK KNOCK
THAT MUST BE HER FAT, LITTLE NIECE NOW! HEE! HEE!
THE DOOR IS OPEN, CHILD!
COME IN!

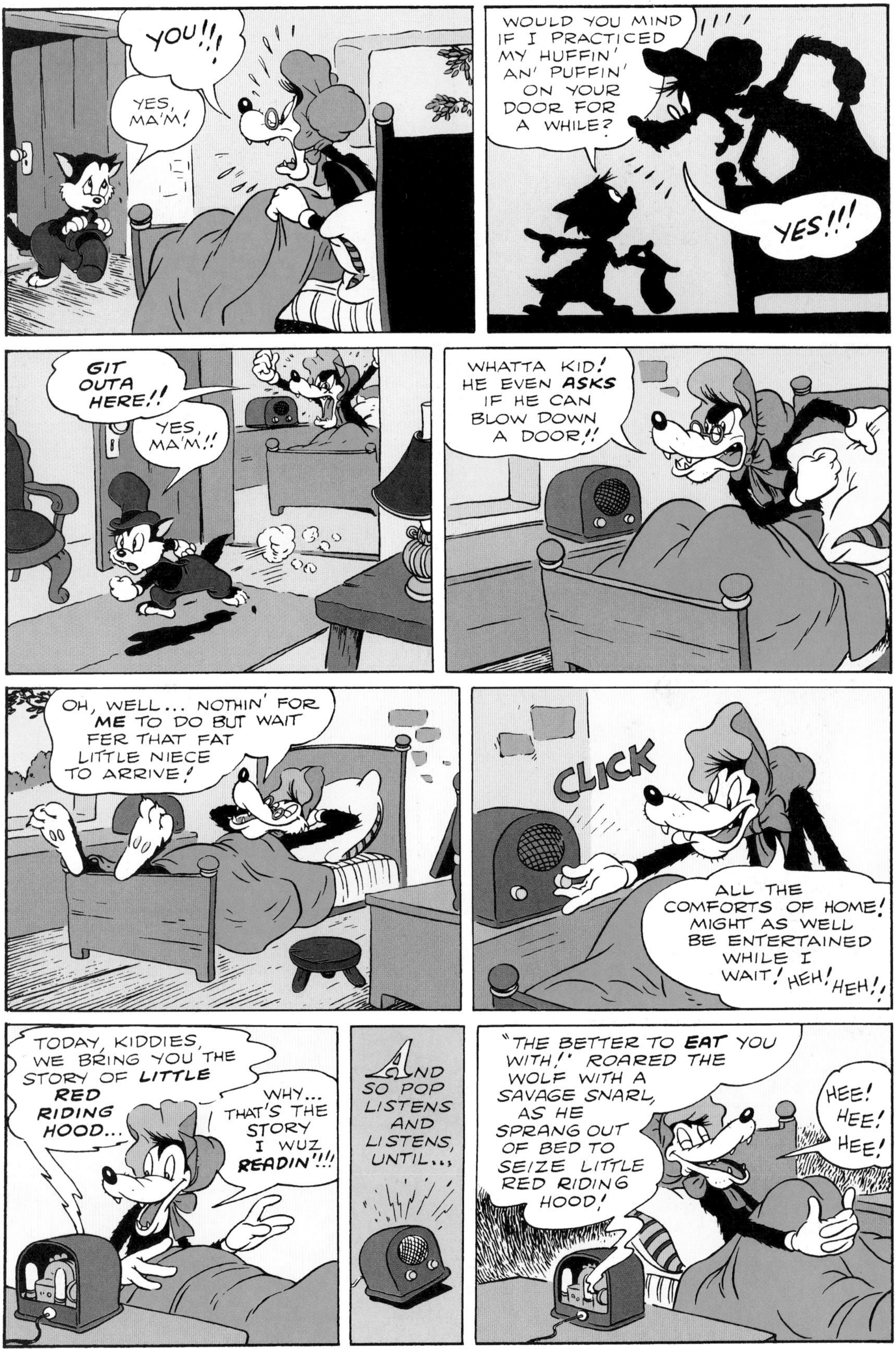
YOU!!!
YES, MA'M!
WOULD YOU MIND IF I PRACTICED MY HUFFIN' AN' PUFFIN' ON YOUR DOOR FOR A WHILE?
YES!!!
GIT OUTA HERE!!
YES, MA'M!!
WHATTA KID! HE EVEN ASKS IF HE CAN BLOW DOWN A DOOR!!
OH, WELL... NOTHIN' FOR ME TO DO BUT WAIT FER THAT FAT LITTLE NIECE TO ARRIVE!
CLICK
ALL THE COMFORTS OF HOME! MIGHT AS WELL BE ENTERTAINED WHILE I WAIT! HEH! HEH!!
TODAY, KIDDIES, WE BRING YOU THE STORY OF LITTLE RED RIDING HOOD...
WHY... THAT'S THE STORY I WUZ READIN'!!!
AND SO POP LISTENS AND LISTENS, UNTIL...
"THE BETTER TO EAT YOU WITH!" ROARED THE WOLF WITH A SAVAGE SNARL, AS HE SPRANG OUT OF BED TO SEIZE LITTLE RED RIDING HOOD!
HEE! HEE! HEE!

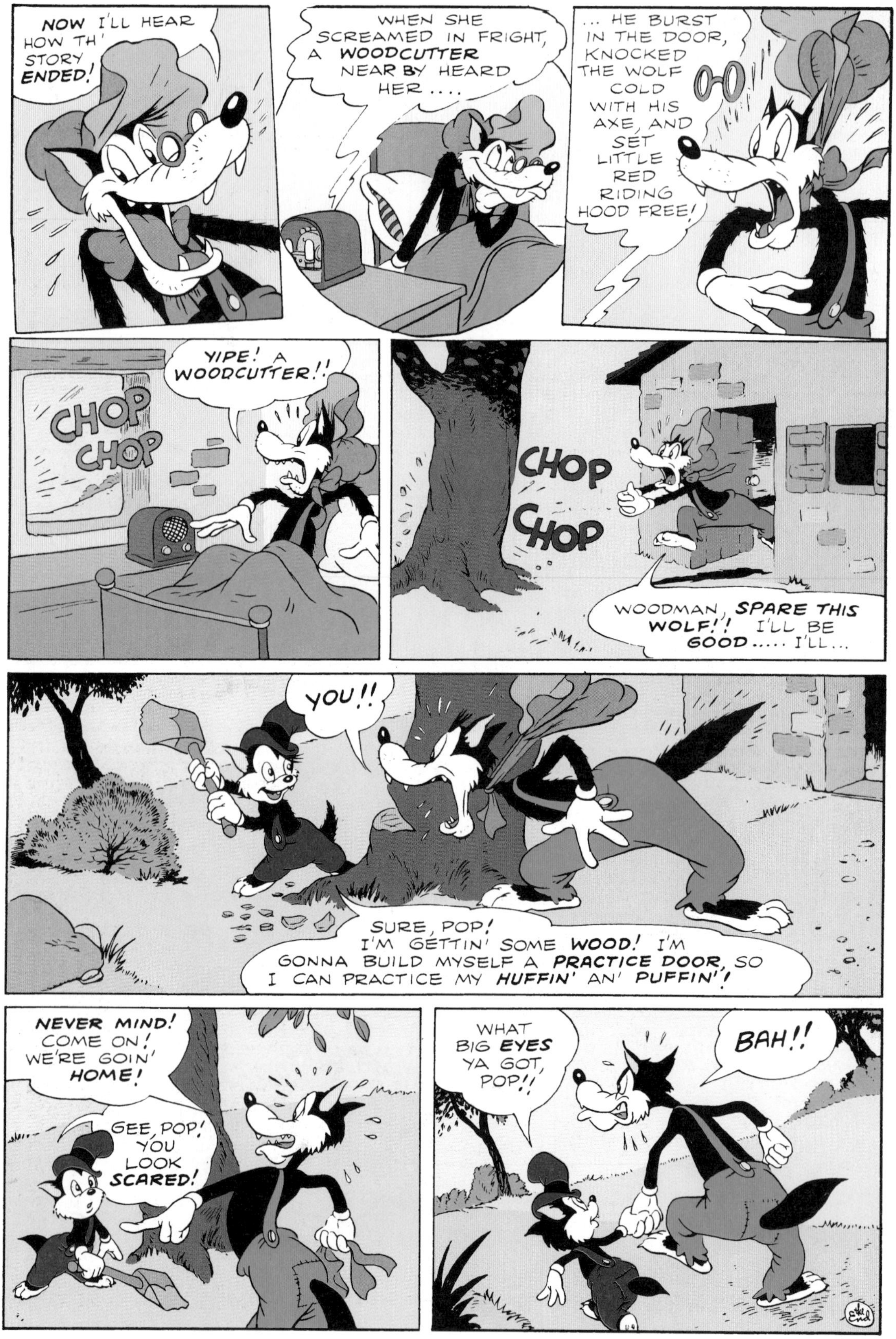
NOW I'LL HEAR HOW TH' STORY ENDED!
WHEN SHE SCREAMED IN FRIGHT, A WOODCUTTER NEAR BY HEARD HER....
... HE BURST IN THE DOOR, KNOCKED THE WOLF COLD WITH HIS AXE, AND SET LITTLE RED RIDING HOOD FREE!
CHOP CHOP
YIPE! A WOODCUTTER!!
CHOP CHOP
WOODMAN, SPARE THIS WOLF!! I'LL BE GOOD..... I'LL...
YOU!!
SURE, POP! I'M GETTIN' SOME WOOD! I'M GONNA BUILD MYSELF A PRACTICE DOOR, SO I CAN PRACTICE MY HUFFIN' AN' PUFFIN'!
NEVER MIND! COME ON! WE'RE GOIN' HOME!
GEE, POP! YOU LOOK SCARED!
WHAT BIG EYES YA GOT, POP!!
BAH!!
The End

Walt Disney's MICKEY MOUSE in STIR CRAZY

NIGHT. FOR MOST, THE DARK IS A TIME OF SPOOKY SHADOWS AND CREEPING UNKNOWNS —

D 2004-206

BUT FOR SOME, THE NIGHT HOLDS NO MYSTERY! IT IS A TIME SPENT ANTICIPATING CRIME —

I *EXPECTED* THAT BIG APE'S ONE-TRACK MIND WOULD LEAD ME HERE!

CUSTOMS CONFISCATION WAREHOUSE

WHILE FOR OTHERS, A TIME OF SINISTER SCHEMES ROUTINELY FOILED —

HAR HAR *HAR!* AIN'T *NOTHIN'* OR *NO ONE* GONNA MESS UP *THIS* SCORE!

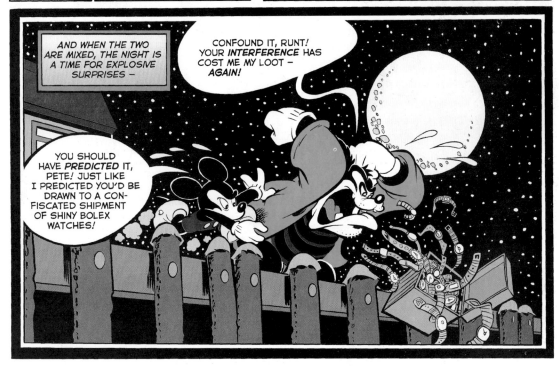

AND WHEN THE TWO ARE MIXED, THE NIGHT IS A TIME FOR EXPLOSIVE SURPRISES —

CONFOUND IT, RUNT! YOUR *INTERFERENCE* HAS COST ME MY LOOT — *AGAIN!*

YOU SHOULD HAVE *PREDICTED* IT, PETE! JUST LIKE I PREDICTED YOU'D BE DRAWN TO A CON-FISCATED SHIPMENT OF SHINY BOLEX WATCHES!

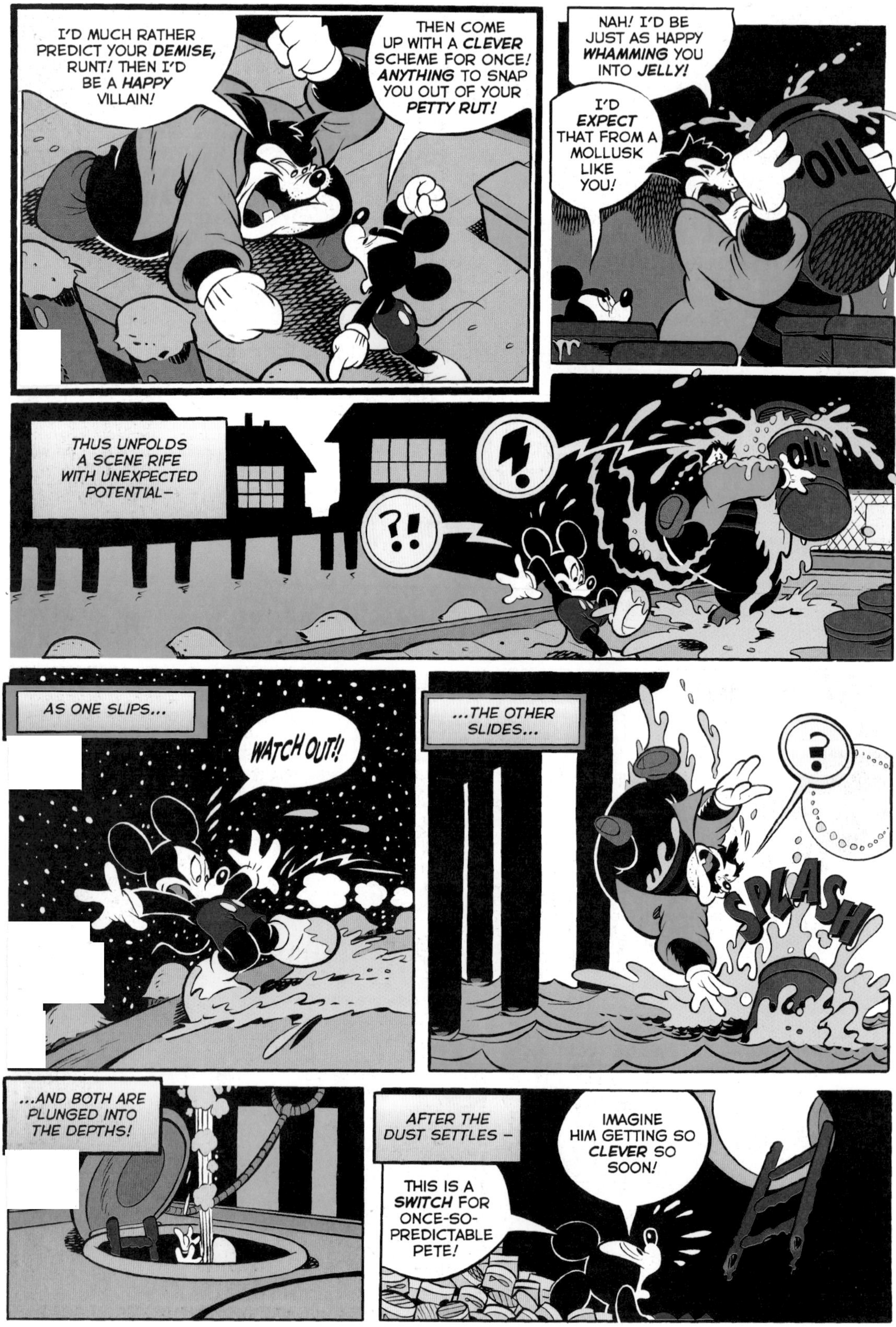

I'D MUCH RATHER PREDICT YOUR DEMISE, RUNT! THEN I'D BE A HAPPY VILLAIN!
THEN COME UP WITH A CLEVER SCHEME FOR ONCE! ANYTHING TO SNAP YOU OUT OF YOUR PETTY RUT!
NAH! I'D BE JUST AS HAPPY WHAMMING YOU INTO JELLY!
I'D EXPECT THAT FROM A MOLLUSK LIKE YOU!
OIL
THUS UNFOLDS A SCENE RIFE WITH UNEXPECTED POTENTIAL—
?!
OIL
AS ONE SLIPS...
WATCH OUT!!
...THE OTHER SLIDES...
?
SPLASH
...AND BOTH ARE PLUNGED INTO THE DEPTHS!
AFTER THE DUST SETTLES —
IMAGINE HIM GETTING SO CLEVER SO SOON!
THIS IS A SWITCH FOR ONCE-SO-PREDICTABLE PETE!

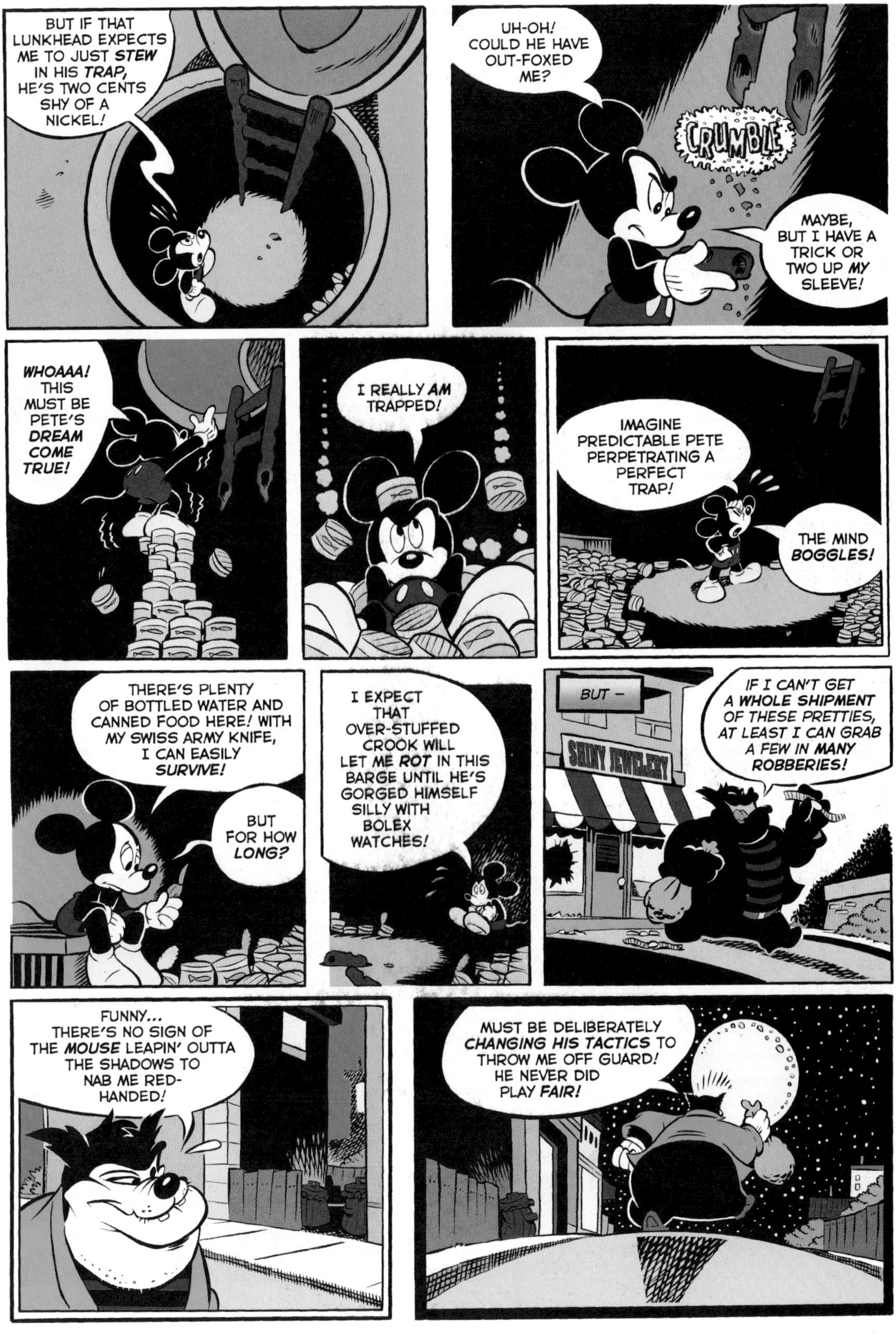

BUT IF THAT LUNKHEAD EXPECTS ME TO JUST STEW IN HIS TRAP, HE'S TWO CENTS SHY OF A NICKEL!
UH-OH! COULD HE HAVE OUT-FOXED ME?
CRUMBLE
MAYBE, BUT I HAVE A TRICK OR TWO UP MY SLEEVE!
WHOAAA! THIS MUST BE PETE'S DREAM COME TRUE!
I REALLY AM TRAPPED!
IMAGINE PREDICTABLE PETE PERPETRATING A PERFECT TRAP!
THE MIND BOGGLES!
THERE'S PLENTY OF BOTTLED WATER AND CANNED FOOD HERE! WITH MY SWISS ARMY KNIFE, I CAN EASILY SURVIVE!
BUT FOR HOW LONG?
I EXPECT THAT OVER-STUFFED CROOK WILL LET ME ROT IN THIS BARGE UNTIL HE'S GORGED HIMSELF SILLY WITH BOLEX WATCHES!
BUT –
SHINY JEWELERY
IF I CAN'T GET A WHOLE SHIPMENT OF THESE PRETTIES, AT LEAST I CAN GRAB A FEW IN MANY ROBBERIES!
FUNNY... THERE'S NO SIGN OF THE MOUSE LEAPIN' OUTTA THE SHADOWS TO NAB ME RED-HANDED!
MUST BE DELIBERATELY CHANGING HIS TACTICS TO THROW ME OFF GUARD! HE NEVER DID PLAY FAIR!

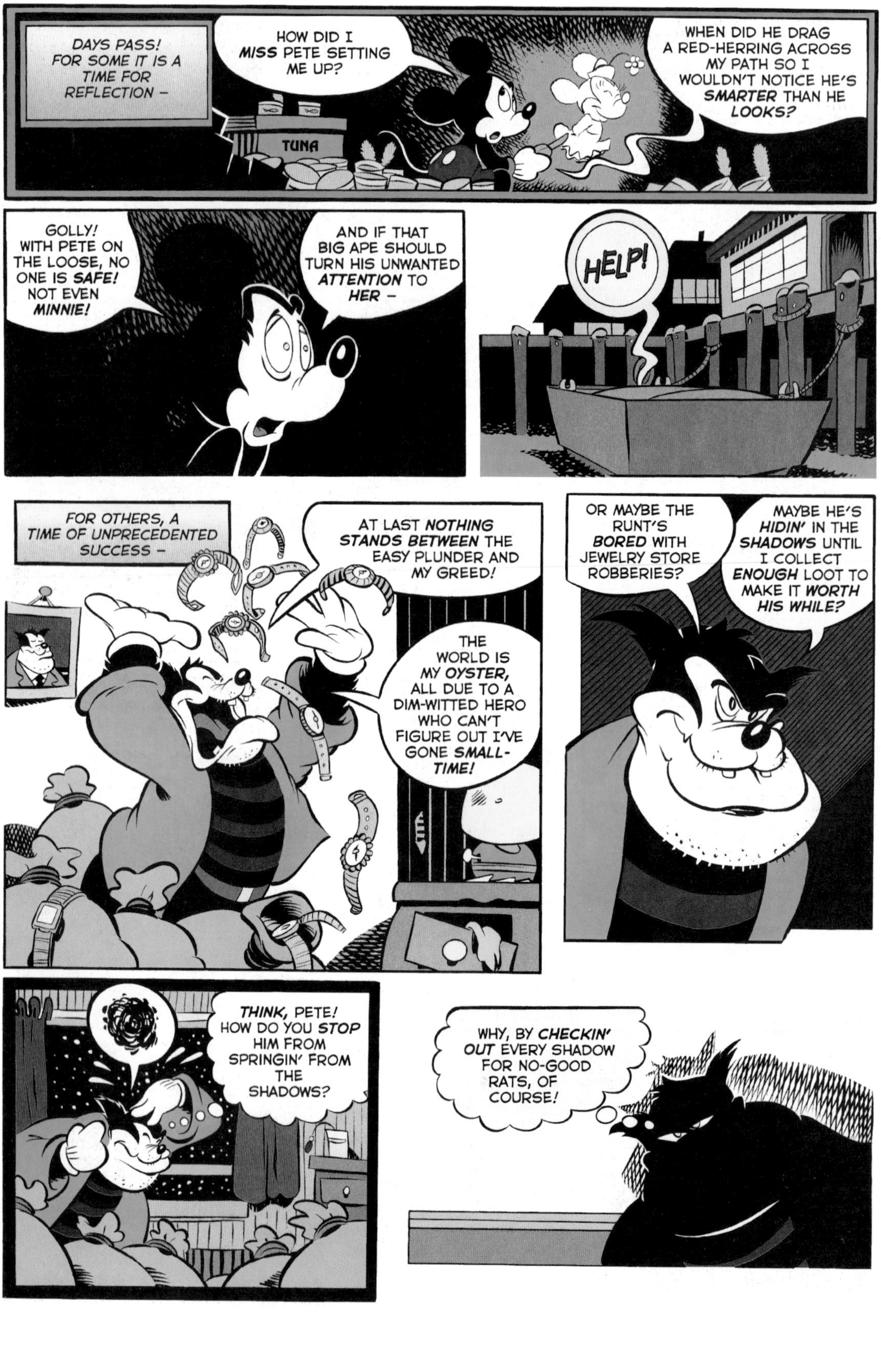
DAYS PASS! FOR SOME IT IS A TIME FOR REFLECTION –
HOW DID I MISS PETE SETTING ME UP?
WHEN DID HE DRAG A RED-HERRING ACROSS MY PATH SO I WOULDN'T NOTICE HE'S SMARTER THAN HE LOOKS?
TUNA
GOLLY! WITH PETE ON THE LOOSE, NO ONE IS SAFE! NOT EVEN MINNIE!
AND IF THAT BIG APE SHOULD TURN HIS UNWANTED ATTENTION TO HER –
HELP!
FOR OTHERS, A TIME OF UNPRECEDENTED SUCCESS –
AT LAST NOTHING STANDS BETWEEN THE EASY PLUNDER AND MY GREED!
THE WORLD IS MY OYSTER, ALL DUE TO A DIM-WITTED HERO WHO CAN'T FIGURE OUT I'VE GONE SMALL-TIME!
OR MAYBE THE RUNT'S BORED WITH JEWELRY STORE ROBBERIES?
MAYBE HE'S HIDIN' IN THE SHADOWS UNTIL I COLLECT ENOUGH LOOT TO MAKE IT WORTH HIS WHILE?
THINK, PETE! HOW DO YOU STOP HIM FROM SPRINGIN' FROM THE SHADOWS?
WHY, BY CHECKIN' OUT EVERY SHADOW FOR NO-GOOD RATS, OF COURSE!

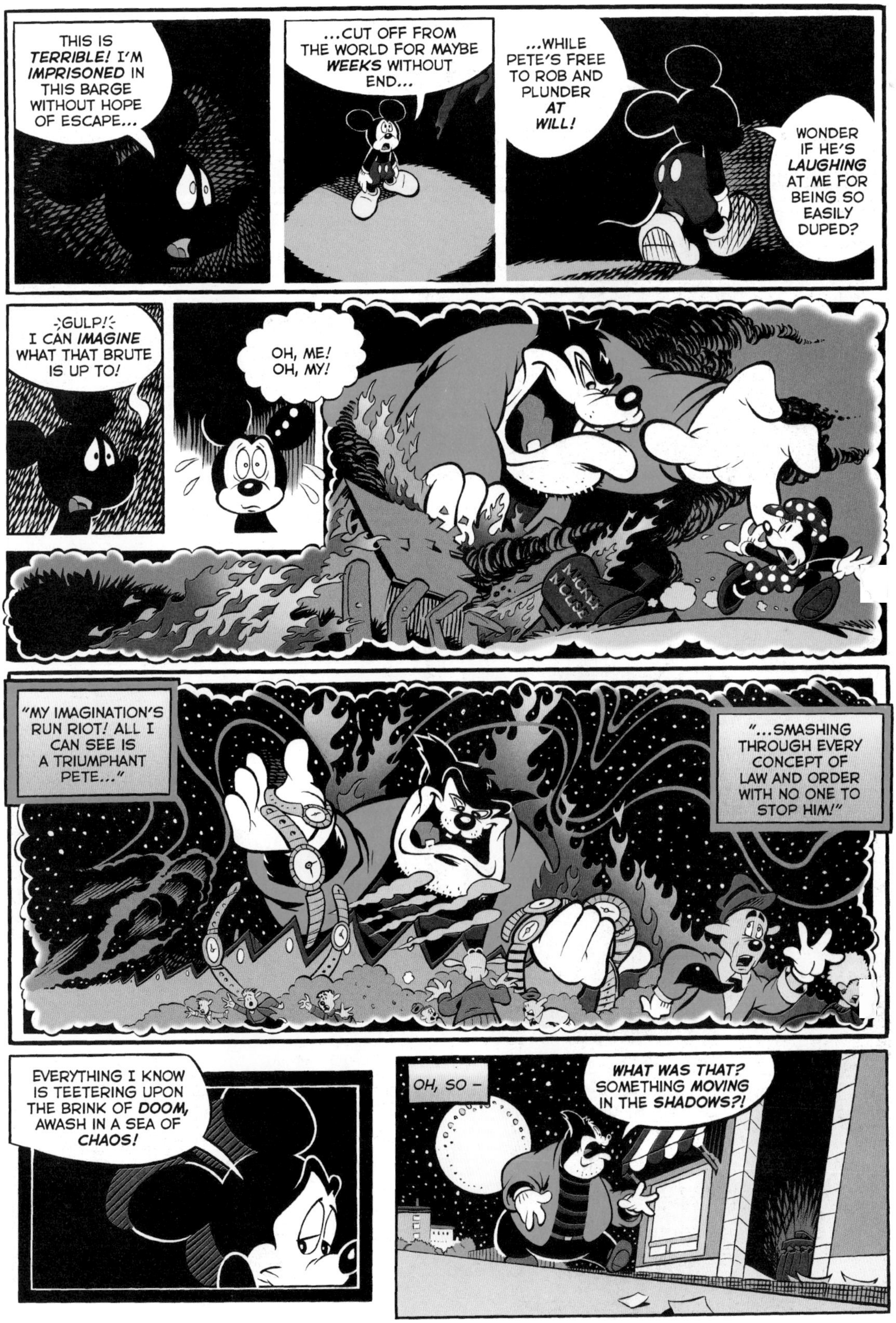
THIS IS TERRIBLE! I'M IMPRISONED IN THIS BARGE WITHOUT HOPE OF ESCAPE...
...CUT OFF FROM THE WORLD FOR MAYBE WEEKS WITHOUT END...
...WHILE PETE'S FREE TO ROB AND PLUNDER AT WILL!
WONDER IF HE'S LAUGHING AT ME FOR BEING SO EASILY DUPED?
GULP! I CAN IMAGINE WHAT THAT BRUTE IS UP TO!
OH, ME! OH, MY!
MICKEY MOUSE
"MY IMAGINATION'S RUN RIOT! ALL I CAN SEE IS A TRIUMPHANT PETE..."
"...SMASHING THROUGH EVERY CONCEPT OF LAW AND ORDER WITH NO ONE TO STOP HIM!"
EVERYTHING I KNOW IS TEETERING UPON THE BRINK OF DOOM, AWASH IN A SEA OF CHAOS!
OH, SO –
WHAT WAS THAT? SOMETHING MOVING IN THE SHADOWS?!

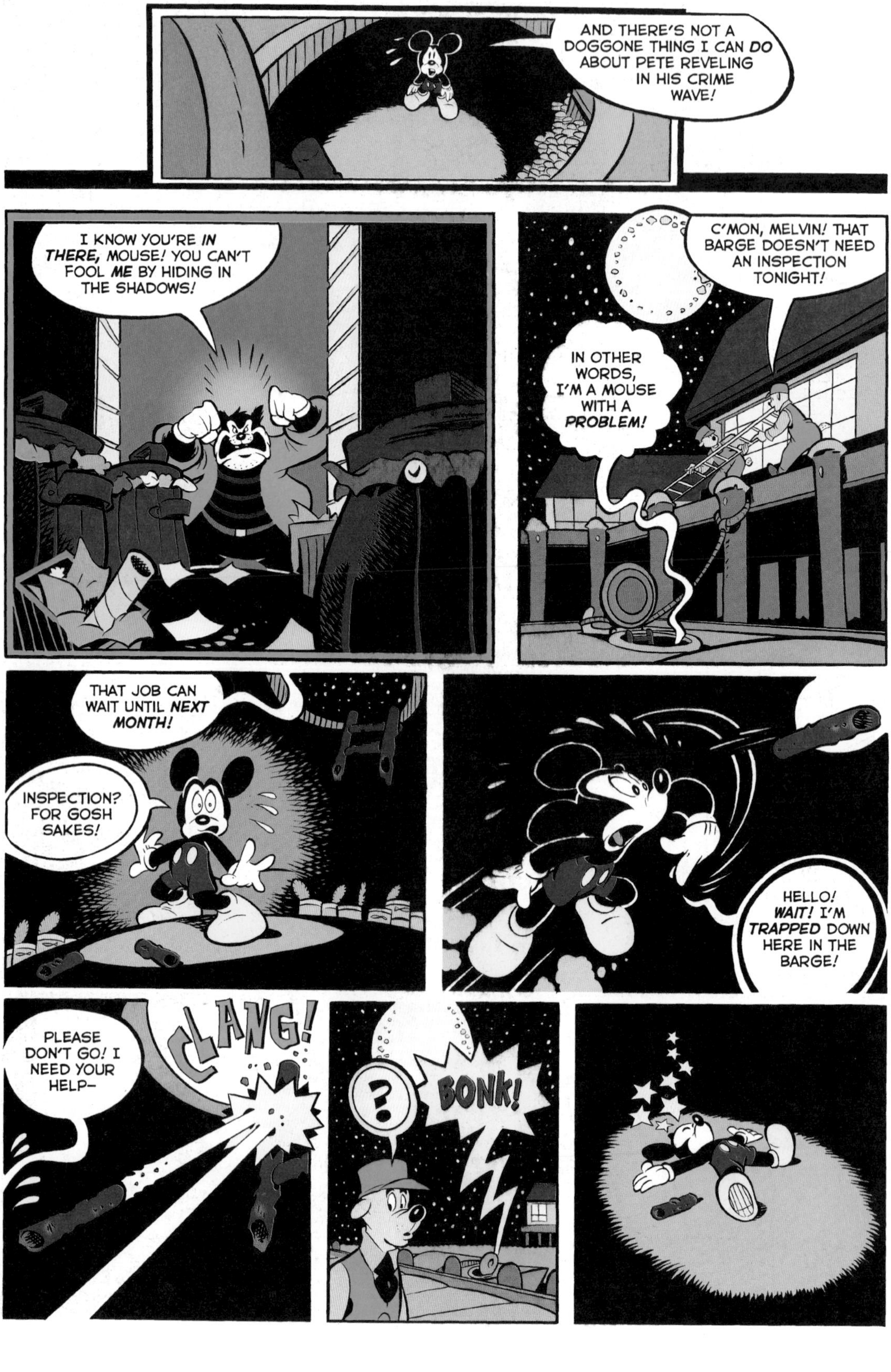
AND THERE'S NOT A DOGGONE THING I CAN DO ABOUT PETE REVELING IN HIS CRIME WAVE!
I KNOW YOU'RE IN THERE, MOUSE! YOU CAN'T FOOL ME BY HIDING IN THE SHADOWS!
C'MON, MELVIN! THAT BARGE DOESN'T NEED AN INSPECTION TONIGHT!
IN OTHER WORDS, I'M A MOUSE WITH A PROBLEM!
THAT JOB CAN WAIT UNTIL NEXT MONTH!
INSPECTION? FOR GOSH SAKES!
HELLO! WAIT! I'M TRAPPED DOWN HERE IN THE BARGE!
PLEASE DON'T GO! I NEED YOUR HELP–
CLANG!
?
BONK!

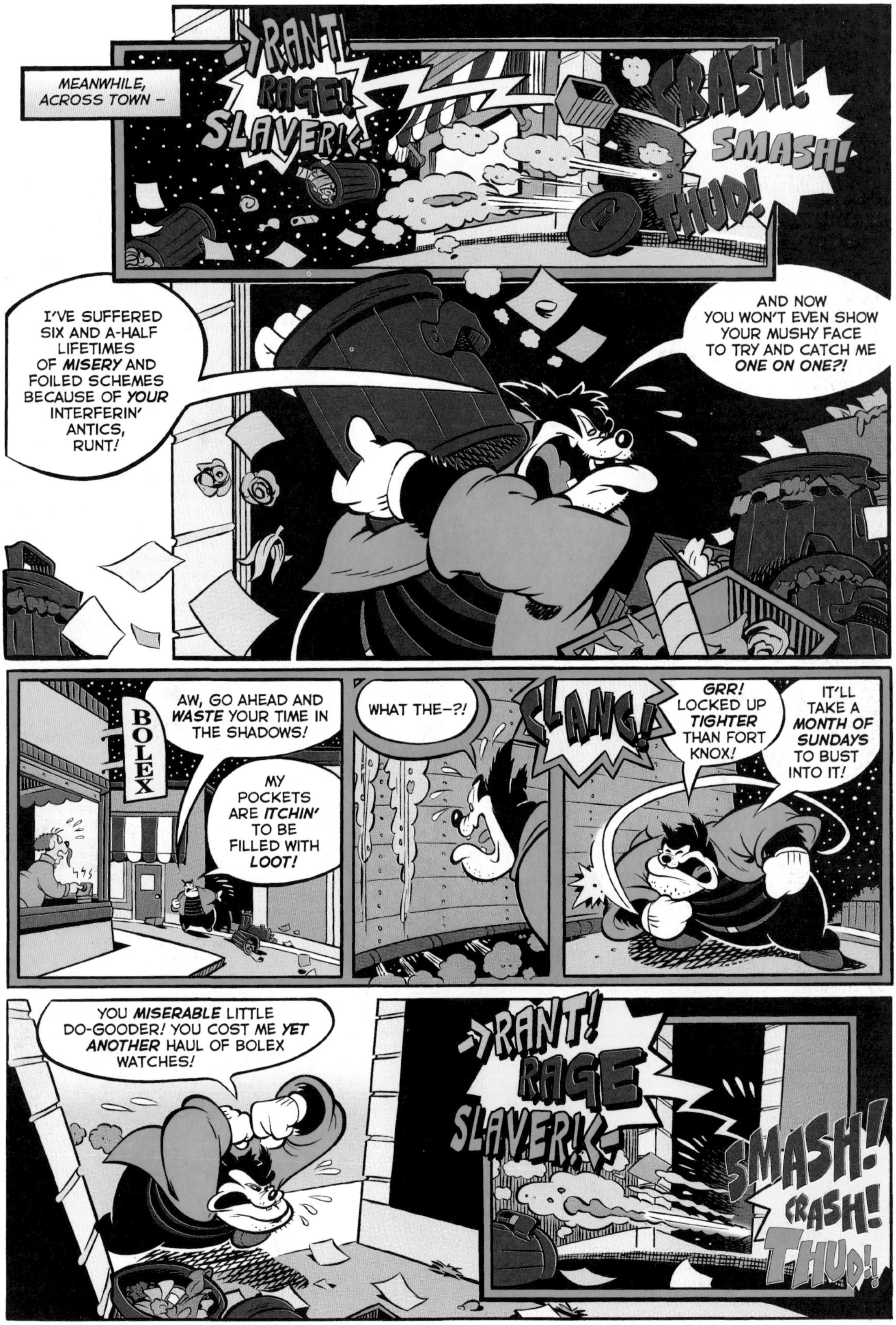
MEANWHILE, ACROSS TOWN –
RANT! RAGE! SLAVER!
CRASH! SMASH! THUD!
I'VE SUFFERED SIX AND A-HALF LIFETIMES OF *MISERY* AND FOILED SCHEMES BECAUSE OF *YOUR* INTERFERIN' ANTICS, RUNT!
AND NOW YOU WON'T EVEN SHOW YOUR MUSHY FACE TO TRY AND CATCH ME *ONE ON ONE?!*
BOLEX
AW, GO AHEAD AND *WASTE* YOUR TIME IN THE SHADOWS!
MY POCKETS ARE *ITCHIN'* TO BE FILLED WITH *LOOT!*
WHAT THE–?!
CLANG!
GRR! LOCKED UP *TIGHTER* THAN FORT KNOX!
IT'LL TAKE A *MONTH OF SUNDAYS* TO BUST INTO IT!
YOU *MISERABLE* LITTLE DO-GOODER! YOU COST ME *YET ANOTHER* HAUL OF BOLEX WATCHES!
RANT! RAGE SLAVER!
SMASH! CRASH! THUD!

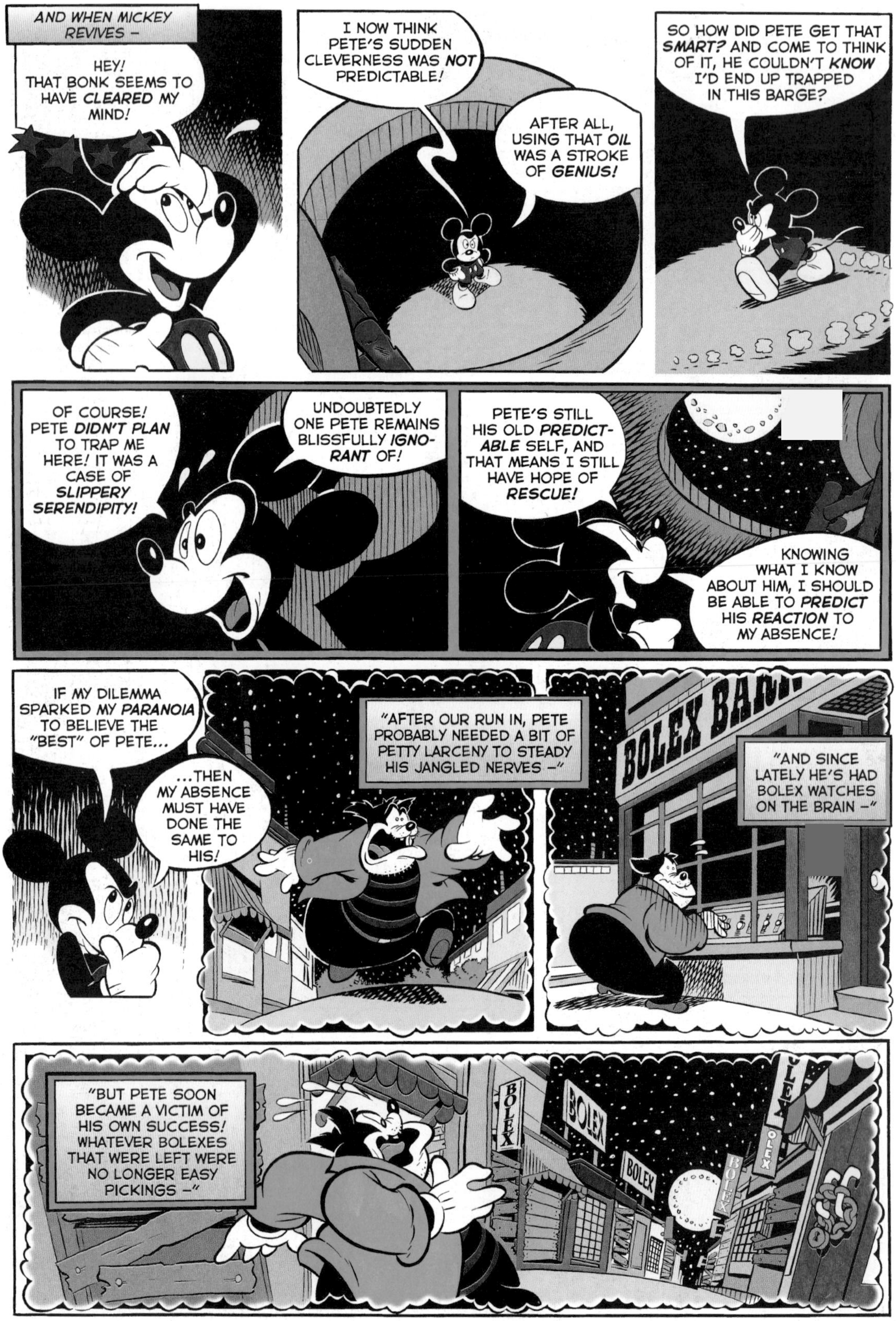
AND WHEN MICKEY REVIVES –
HEY! THAT BONK SEEMS TO HAVE CLEARED MY MIND!
I NOW THINK PETE'S SUDDEN CLEVERNESS WAS NOT PREDICTABLE!
AFTER ALL, USING THAT OIL WAS A STROKE OF GENIUS!
SO HOW DID PETE GET THAT SMART? AND COME TO THINK OF IT, HE COULDN'T KNOW I'D END UP TRAPPED IN THIS BARGE?
OF COURSE! PETE DIDN'T PLAN TO TRAP ME HERE! IT WAS A CASE OF SLIPPERY SERENDIPITY!
UNDOUBTEDLY ONE PETE REMAINS BLISSFULLY IGNORANT OF!
PETE'S STILL HIS OLD PREDICTABLE SELF, AND THAT MEANS I STILL HAVE HOPE OF RESCUE!
KNOWING WHAT I KNOW ABOUT HIM, I SHOULD BE ABLE TO PREDICT HIS REACTION TO MY ABSENCE!
IF MY DILEMMA SPARKED MY PARANOIA TO BELIEVE THE "BEST" OF PETE...
...THEN MY ABSENCE MUST HAVE DONE THE SAME TO HIS!
"AFTER OUR RUN IN, PETE PROBABLY NEEDED A BIT OF PETTY LARCENY TO STEADY HIS JANGLED NERVES –"
BOLEX
"AND SINCE LATELY HE'S HAD BOLEX WATCHES ON THE BRAIN –"
"BUT PETE SOON BECAME A VICTIM OF HIS OWN SUCCESS! WHATEVER BOLEXES THAT WERE LEFT WERE NO LONGER EASY PICKINGS –"
BOLEX
BOLEX
BOLEX
BOLEX

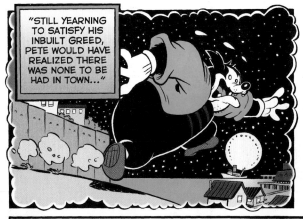

"STILL YEARNING TO SATISFY HIS INBUILT GREED, PETE WOULD HAVE REALIZED THERE WAS NONE TO BE HAD IN TOWN..."

...AND WOULD HAVE RETRACED HIS STEPS TO SCORES THAT *GOT AWAY* FROM HIM—LIKE THE HEIST I *FOILED* HERE ON THE WATERFRONT!

"PREDICTABLE PETE WOULD SKULK BACK TO THE SAME DOCK TO PILLAGE THE SAME SHIPMENT OF CONFISCATED BOLEX WATCHES –"

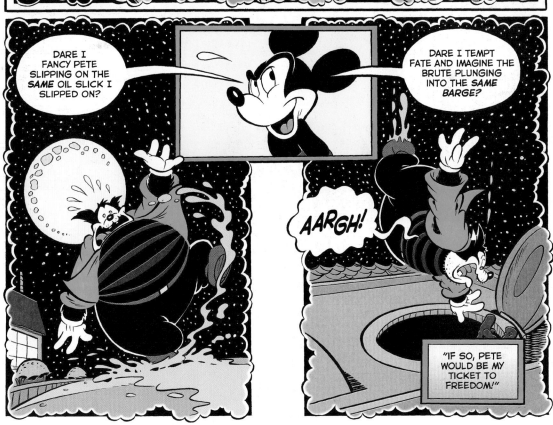

DARE I FANCY PETE SLIPPING ON THE *SAME OIL SLICK* I SLIPPED ON?

DARE I TEMPT FATE AND IMAGINE THE BRUTE PLUNGING INTO THE *SAME BARGE?*

AARGH!

"IF SO, PETE WOULD BE MY TICKET TO FREEDOM!"

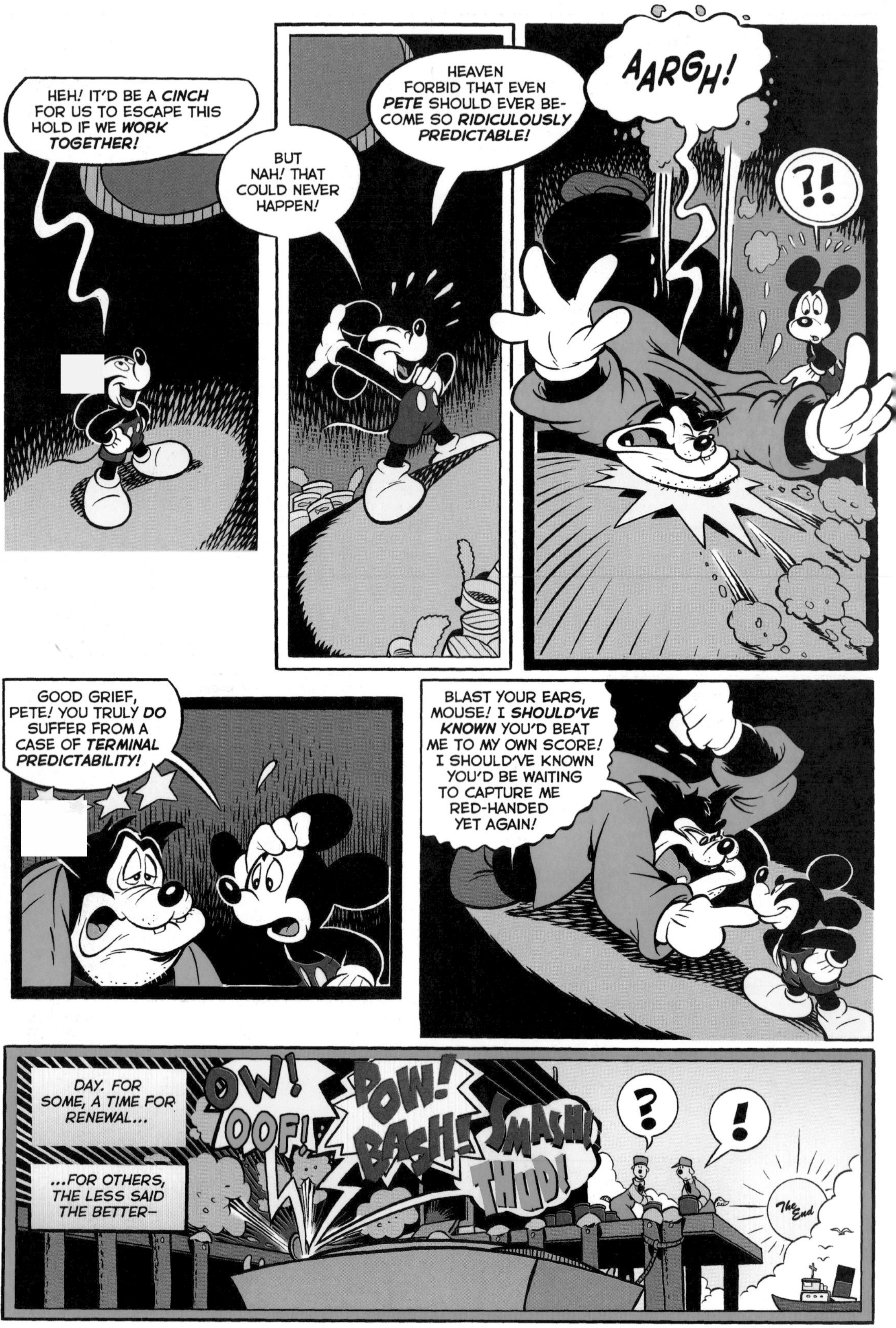

HEH! IT'D BE A CINCH FOR US TO ESCAPE THIS HOLD IF WE WORK TOGETHER!
BUT NAH! THAT COULD NEVER HAPPEN!
HEAVEN FORBID THAT EVEN PETE SHOULD EVER BE-COME SO RIDICULOUSLY PREDICTABLE!
AARGH!
?!
GOOD GRIEF, PETE! YOU TRULY DO SUFFER FROM A CASE OF TERMINAL PREDICTABILITY!
BLAST YOUR EARS, MOUSE! I SHOULD'VE KNOWN YOU'D BEAT ME TO MY OWN SCORE! I SHOULD'VE KNOWN YOU'D BE WAITING TO CAPTURE ME RED-HANDED YET AGAIN!
DAY. FOR SOME, A TIME FOR RENEWAL...
...FOR OTHERS, THE LESS SAID THE BETTER–
OW!
OOF!
POW!
BASH!
SMASH!
THUD!
?
!
The End

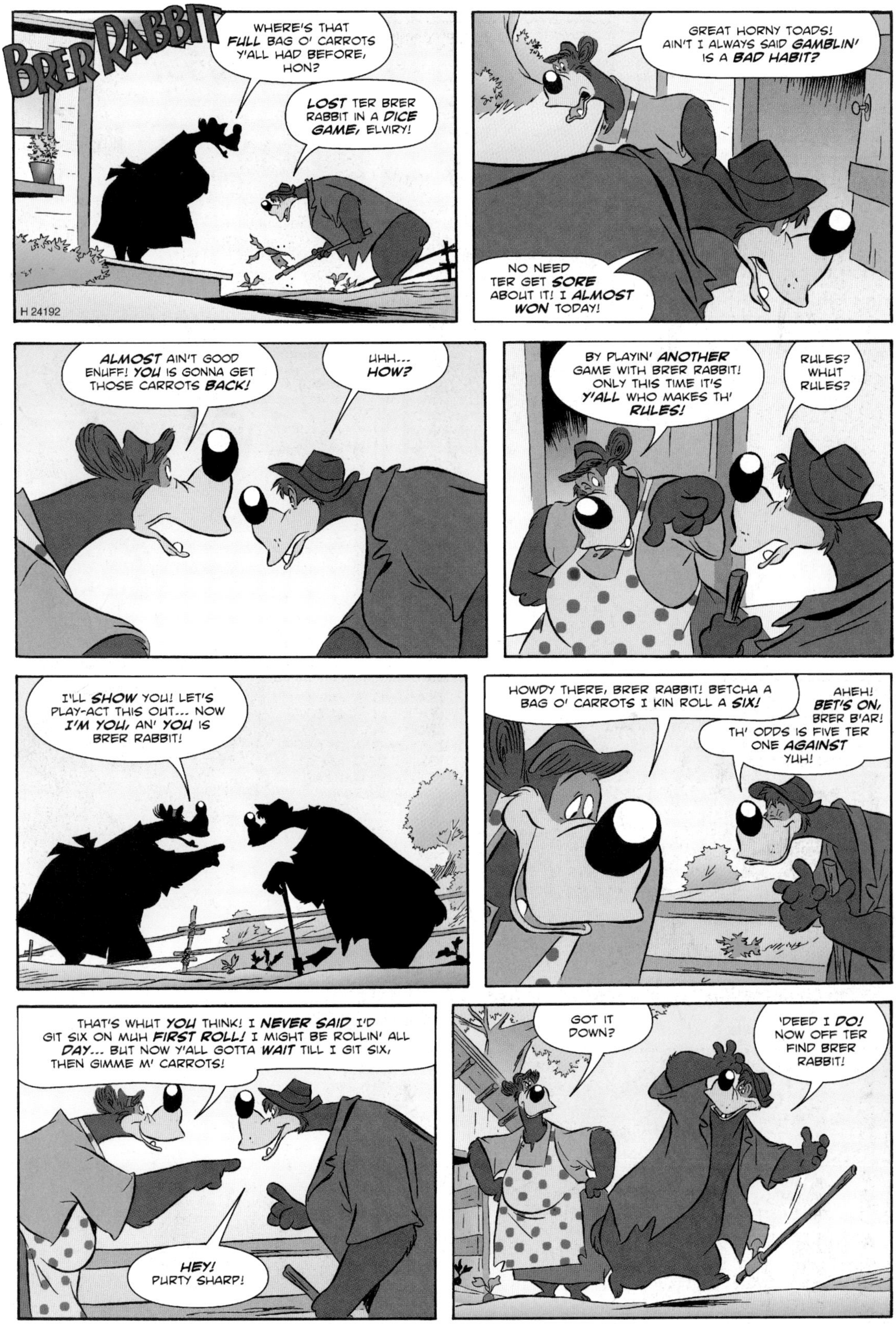
BRER RABBIT
WHERE'S THAT FULL BAG O' CARROTS Y'ALL HAD BEFORE, HON?
LOST TER BRER RABBIT IN A DICE GAME, ELVIRY!
H 24192
GREAT HORNY TOADS! AIN'T I ALWAYS SAID GAMBLIN' IS A BAD HABIT?
NO NEED TER GET SORE ABOUT IT! I ALMOST WON TODAY!
ALMOST AIN'T GOOD ENUFF! YOU IS GONNA GET THOSE CARROTS BACK!
UHH... HOW?
BY PLAYIN' ANOTHER GAME WITH BRER RABBIT! ONLY THIS TIME IT'S Y'ALL WHO MAKES TH' RULES!
RULES? WHUT RULES?
I'LL SHOW YOU! LET'S PLAY-ACT THIS OUT... NOW I'M YOU, AN' YOU IS BRER RABBIT!
HOWDY THERE, BRER RABBIT! BETCHA A BAG O' CARROTS I KIN ROLL A SIX!
AHEH! BET'S ON, BRER B'AR!
TH' ODDS IS FIVE TER ONE AGAINST YUH!
THAT'S WHUT YOU THINK! I NEVER SAID I'D GIT SIX ON MUH FIRST ROLL! I MIGHT BE ROLLIN' ALL DAY... BUT NOW Y'ALL GOTTA WAIT TILL I GIT SIX, THEN GIMME M' CARROTS!
HEY! PURTY SHARP!
GOT IT DOWN?
'DEED I DO! NOW OFF TER FIND BRER RABBIT!

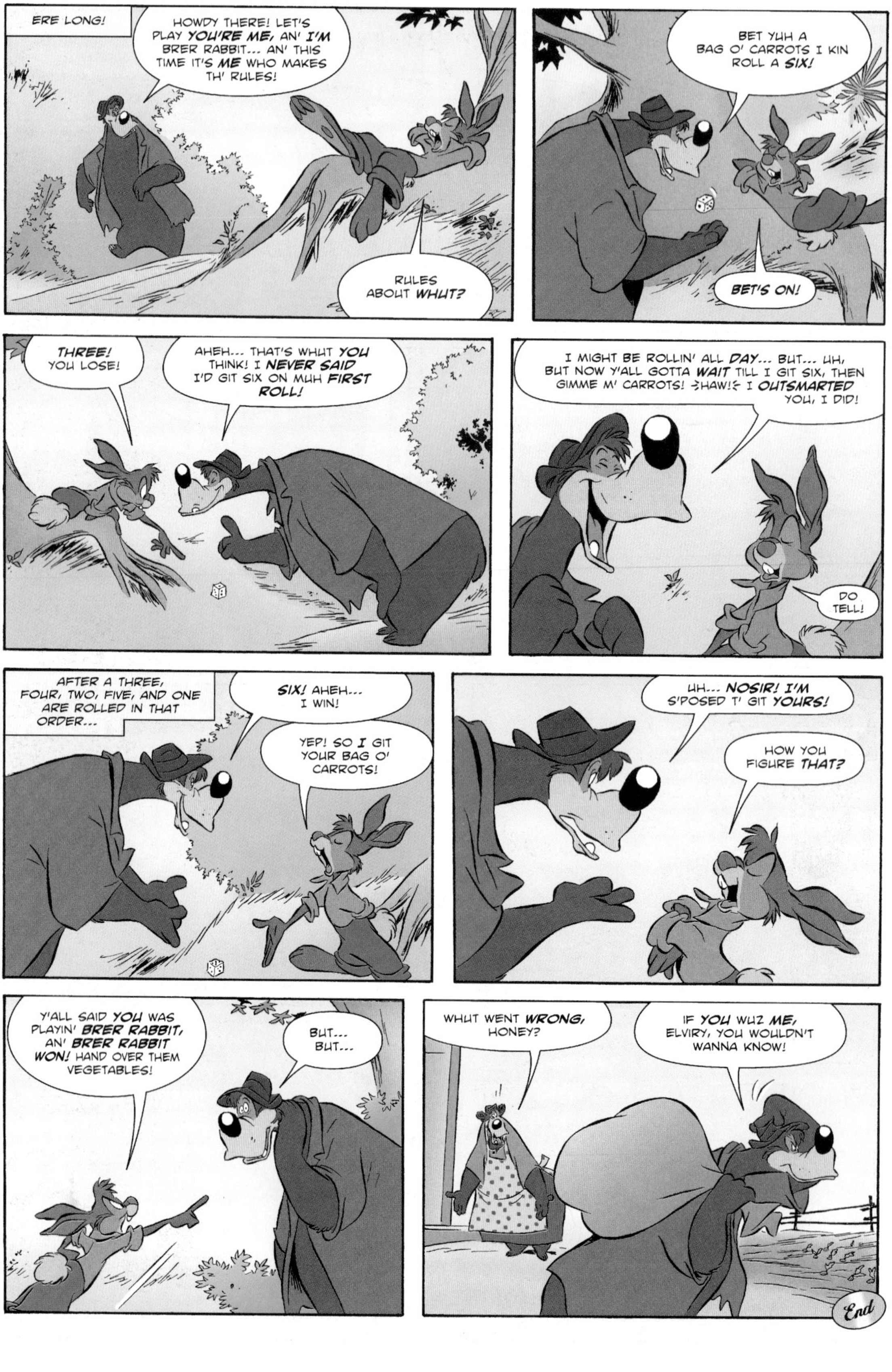

ERE LONG!
HOWDY THERE! LET'S PLAY YOU'RE ME, AN' I'M BRER RABBIT... AN' THIS TIME IT'S ME WHO MAKES TH' RULES!
RULES ABOUT WHUT?
BET YUH A BAG O' CARROTS I KIN ROLL A SIX!
BET'S ON!
THREE! YOU LOSE!
AHEH... THAT'S WHUT YOU THINK! I NEVER SAID I'D GIT SIX ON MUH FIRST ROLL!
I MIGHT BE ROLLIN' ALL DAY... BUT... UH, BUT NOW Y'ALL GOTTA WAIT TILL I GIT SIX, THEN GIMME M' CARROTS! HAW! I OUTSMARTED YOU, I DID!
DO TELL!
AFTER A THREE, FOUR, TWO, FIVE, AND ONE ARE ROLLED IN THAT ORDER...
SIX! AHEH... I WIN!
YEP! SO I GIT YOUR BAG O' CARROTS!
UH... NOSIR! I'M S'POSED T' GIT YOURS!
HOW YOU FIGURE THAT?
Y'ALL SAID YOU WAS PLAYIN' BRER RABBIT, AN' BRER RABBIT WON! HAND OVER THEM VEGETABLES!
BUT... BUT...
WHUT WENT WRONG, HONEY?
IF YOU WUZ ME, ELVIRY, YOU WOULDN'T WANNA KNOW!
End

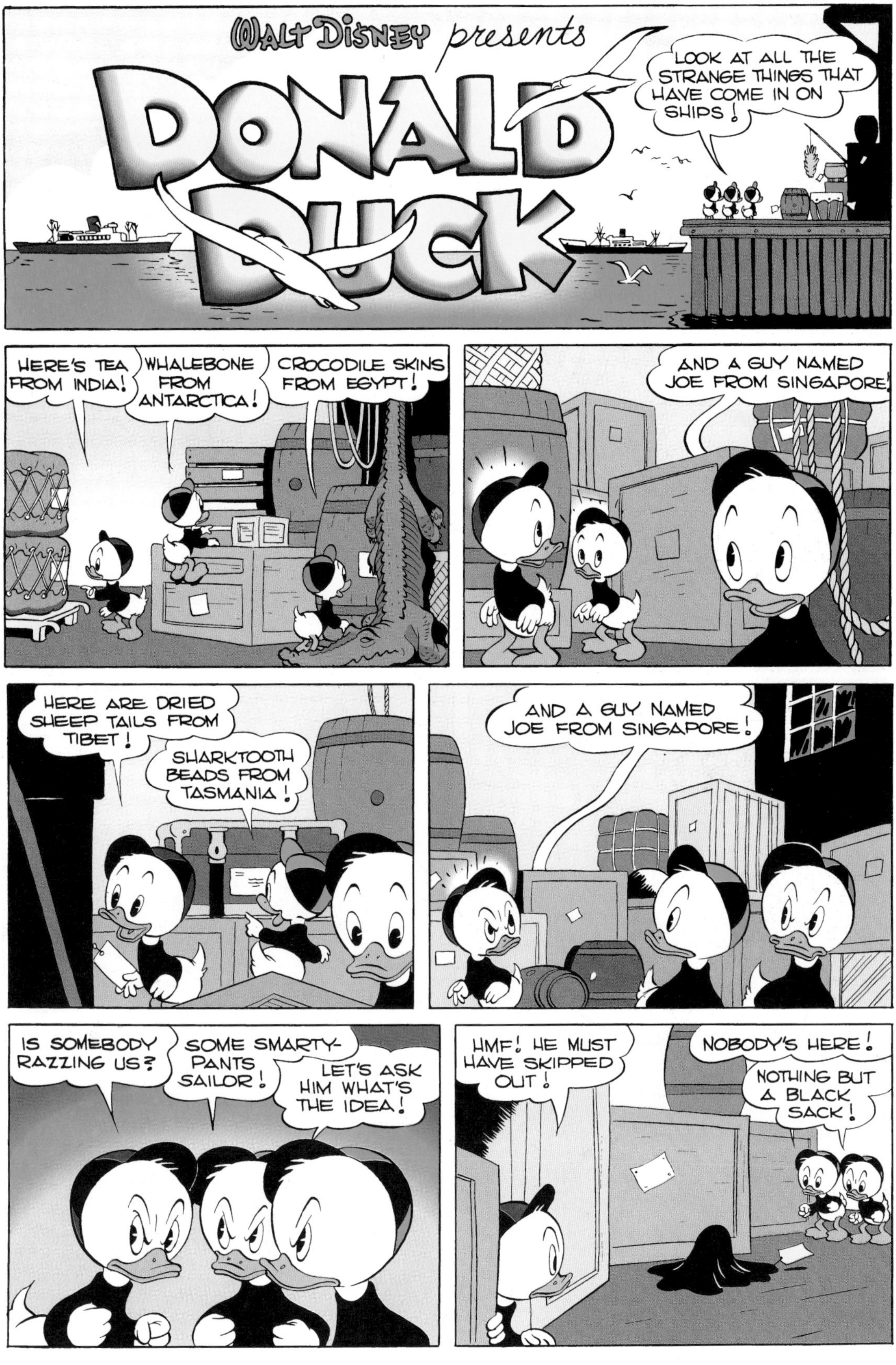
WALT DISNEY presents
DONALD DUCK
LOOK AT ALL THE STRANGE THINGS THAT HAVE COME IN ON SHIPS!
HERE'S TEA FROM INDIA!
WHALEBONE FROM ANTARCTICA!
CROCODILE SKINS FROM EGYPT!
AND A GUY NAMED JOE FROM SINGAPORE!
HERE ARE DRIED SHEEP TAILS FROM TIBET!
SHARKTOOTH BEADS FROM TASMANIA!
AND A GUY NAMED JOE FROM SINGAPORE!
IS SOMEBODY RAZZING US?
SOME SMARTY-PANTS SAILOR!
LET'S ASK HIM WHAT'S THE IDEA!
HMF! HE MUST HAVE SKIPPED OUT!
NOBODY'S HERE!
NOTHING BUT A BLACK SACK!

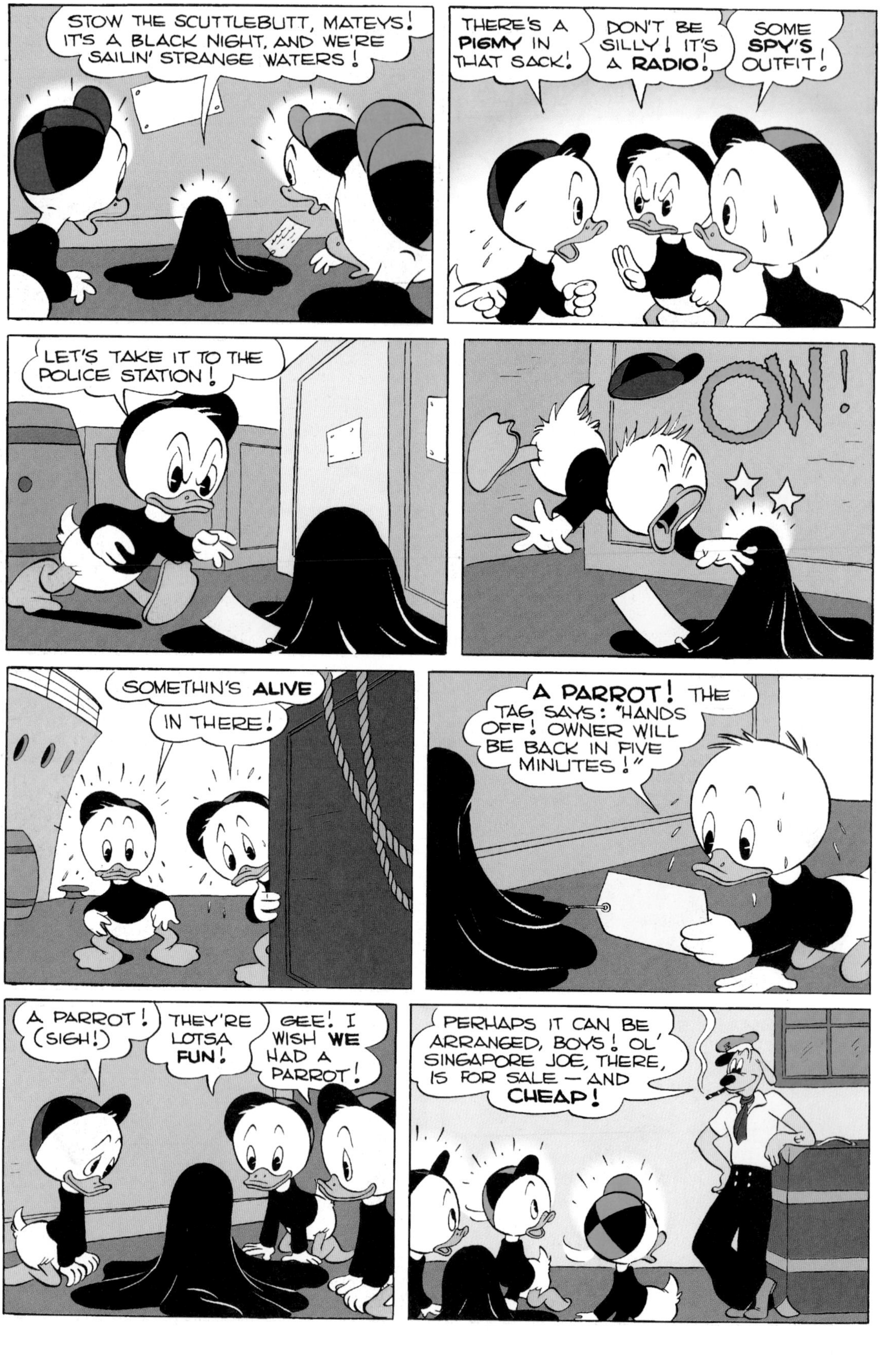
STOW THE SCUTTLEBUTT, MATEYS! IT'S A BLACK NIGHT, AND WE'RE SAILIN' STRANGE WATERS!
THERE'S A PIGMY IN THAT SACK!
DON'T BE SILLY! IT'S A RADIO!
SOME SPY'S OUTFIT!
LET'S TAKE IT TO THE POLICE STATION!
OW!
SOMETHIN'S ALIVE
IN THERE!
A PARROT! THE TAG SAYS: "HANDS OFF! OWNER WILL BE BACK IN FIVE MINUTES!"
A PARROT! (SIGH!)
THEY'RE LOTSA FUN!
GEE! I WISH WE HAD A PARROT!
PERHAPS IT CAN BE ARRANGED, BOYS! OL' SINGAPORE JOE, THERE, IS FOR SALE — AND CHEAP!

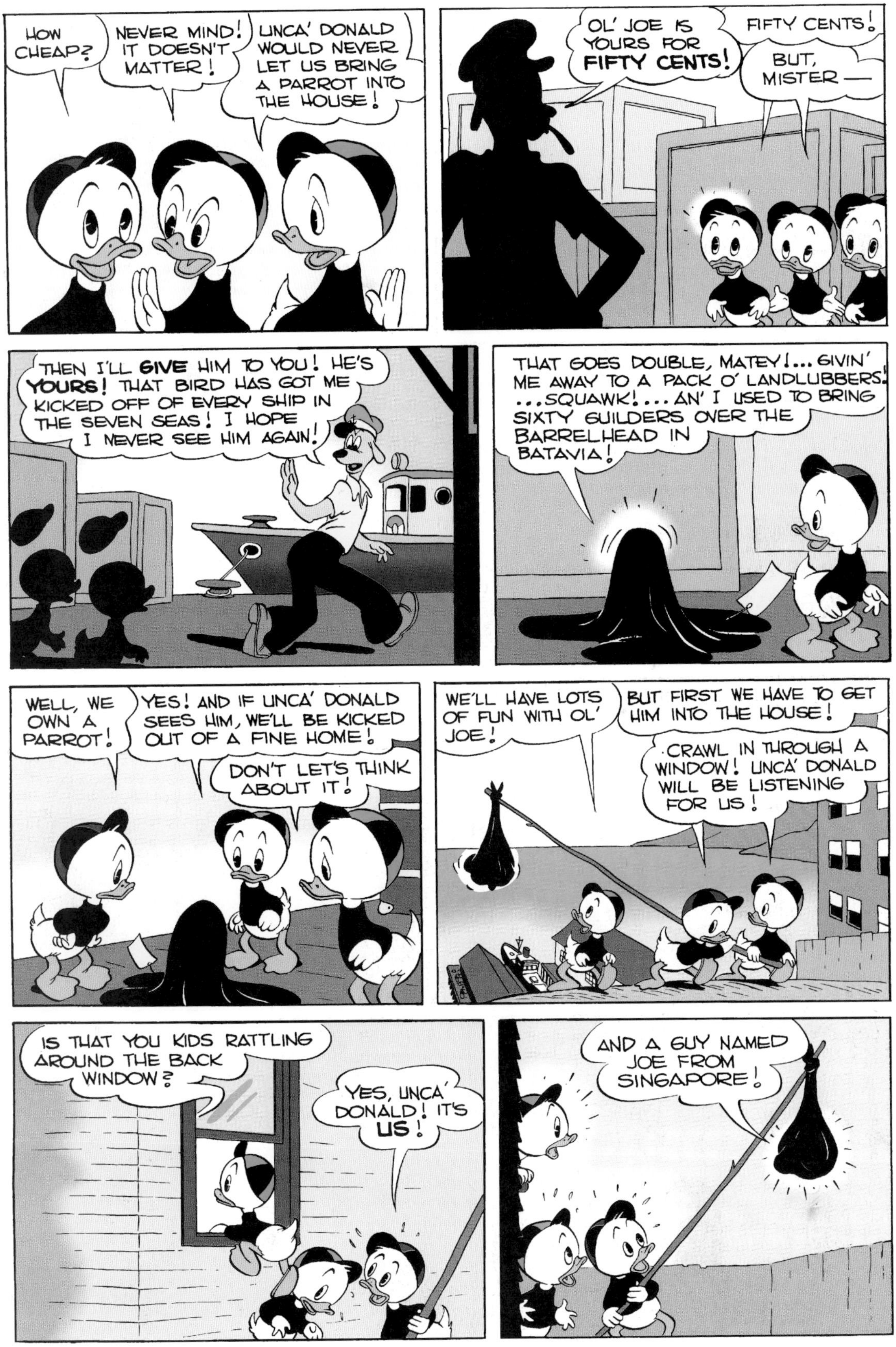

HOW CHEAP?
NEVER MIND! IT DOESN'T MATTER!
UNCA' DONALD WOULD NEVER LET US BRING A PARROT INTO THE HOUSE!
OL' JOE IS YOURS FOR **FIFTY CENTS!**
FIFTY CENTS!
BUT, MISTER —
THEN I'LL **GIVE** HIM TO YOU! HE'S **YOURS!** THAT BIRD HAS GOT ME KICKED OFF OF EVERY SHIP IN THE SEVEN SEAS! I HOPE I NEVER SEE HIM AGAIN!
THAT GOES DOUBLE, MATEY!... GIVIN' ME AWAY TO A PACK O' LANDLUBBERS! ...SQUAWK!... AN' I USED TO BRING SIXTY GUILDERS OVER THE BARRELHEAD IN BATAVIA!
WELL, WE OWN A PARROT!
YES! AND IF UNCA' DONALD SEES HIM, WE'LL BE KICKED OUT OF A FINE HOME!
DON'T LET'S THINK ABOUT IT!
WE'LL HAVE LOTS OF FUN WITH OL' JOE!
BUT FIRST WE HAVE TO GET HIM INTO THE HOUSE!
CRAWL IN THROUGH A WINDOW! UNCA' DONALD WILL BE LISTENING FOR US!
IS THAT YOU KIDS RATTLING AROUND THE BACK WINDOW?
YES, UNCA' DONALD! IT'S **US!**
AND A GUY NAMED JOE FROM SINGAPORE!

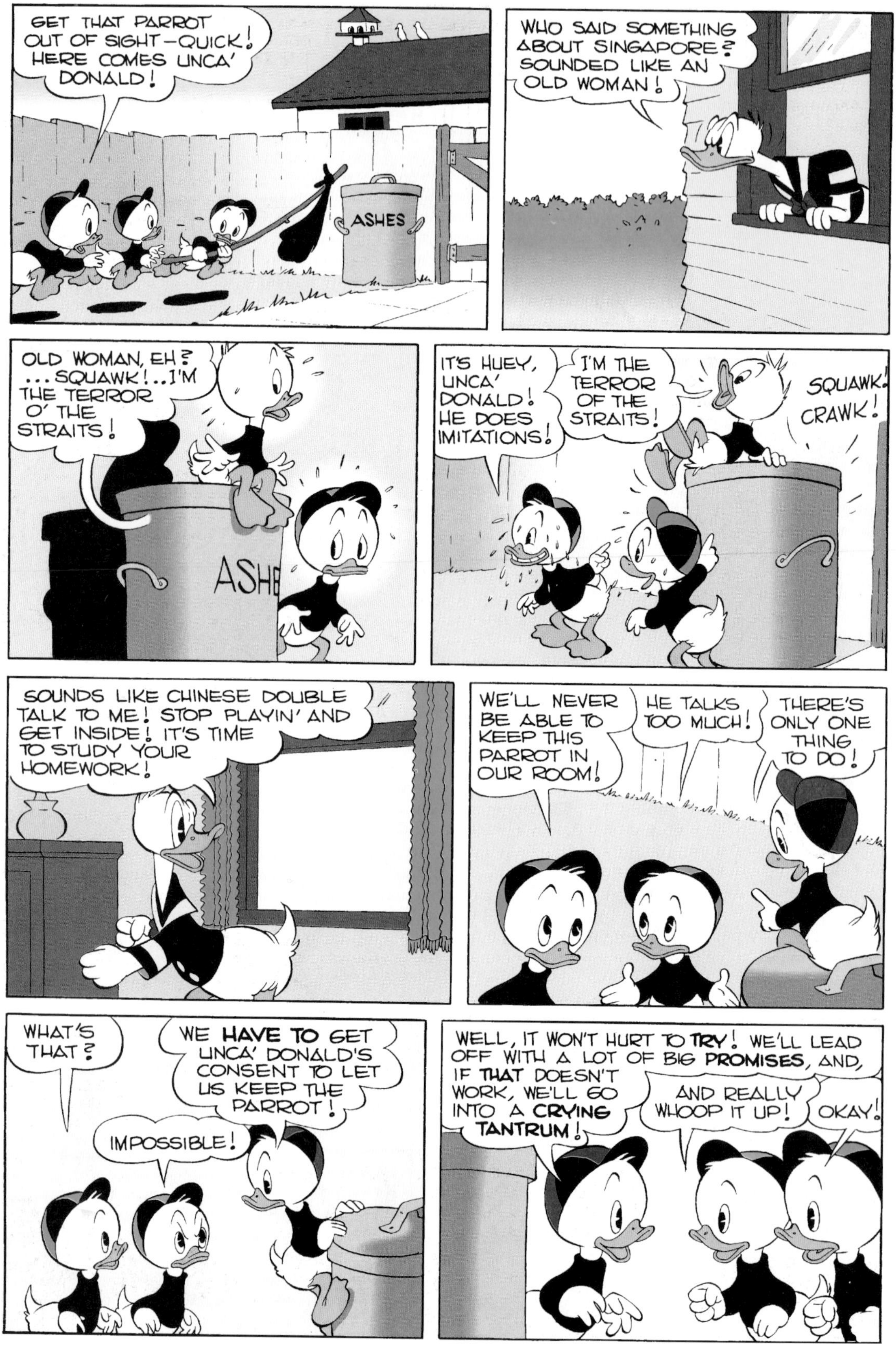
GET THAT PARROT OUT OF SIGHT—QUICK! HERE COMES UNCA' DONALD!
ASHES
WHO SAID SOMETHING ABOUT SINGAPORE? SOUNDED LIKE AN OLD WOMAN!
OLD WOMAN, EH? ... SQUAWK!...I'M THE TERROR O' THE STRAITS!
IT'S HUEY, UNCA' DONALD! HE DOES IMITATIONS!
I'M THE TERROR OF THE STRAITS!
SQUAWK! CRAWK!
SOUNDS LIKE CHINESE DOUBLE TALK TO ME! STOP PLAYIN' AND GET INSIDE! IT'S TIME TO STUDY YOUR HOMEWORK!
WE'LL NEVER BE ABLE TO KEEP THIS PARROT IN OUR ROOM!
HE TALKS TOO MUCH!
THERE'S ONLY ONE THING TO DO!
WHAT'S THAT?
WE HAVE TO GET UNCA' DONALD'S CONSENT TO LET US KEEP THE PARROT!
IMPOSSIBLE!
WELL, IT WON'T HURT TO TRY! WE'LL LEAD OFF WITH A LOT OF BIG PROMISES, AND, IF THAT DOESN'T WORK, WE'LL GO INTO A CRYING TANTRUM!
AND REALLY WHOOP IT UP!
OKAY!

THE KIDS LEAVE OLD JOE HIDDEN IN THE ASH CAN AND GO IN THE HOUSE TO BEARD FEROCIOUS DONALD IN HIS DEN!

UNCA' DONALD, IF WE PROMISE TO MOW THE LAWN AND TRIM THE HEDGE AND WASH THE DISHES AND SWEEP THE FLOORS AND MAKE THE BEDS, MAY WE —

NO!

MAY WE ASK A TEENIE WEENIE LITTLE BITTY FAVOR?

NO!

WE'D LIKE YOU TO LET US KEEP A PARROT!

WHAT? NO!

WAA! BAW! SOB!

WAW! BAW! SOB! WAA!

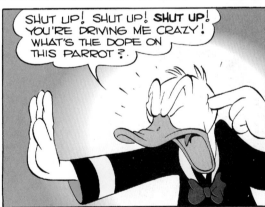

SHUT UP! SHUT UP! SHUT UP! YOU'RE DRIVING ME CRAZY! WHAT'S THE DOPE ON THIS PARROT?

WE'VE GOT — I MEAN, WE CAN GET A PARROT!

FOR ALMOST NOTHING! AND HE —!

IS HE A WELL-MANNERED PARROT?

OH, YES! YES, INDEED!

HE TALKS LIKE A COLLEGE MAN — ALMOST!

AND HE'S AS GENTLE AS A DOVE —!

WELL, IF HE'S AS GOOD AS YOU SAY —

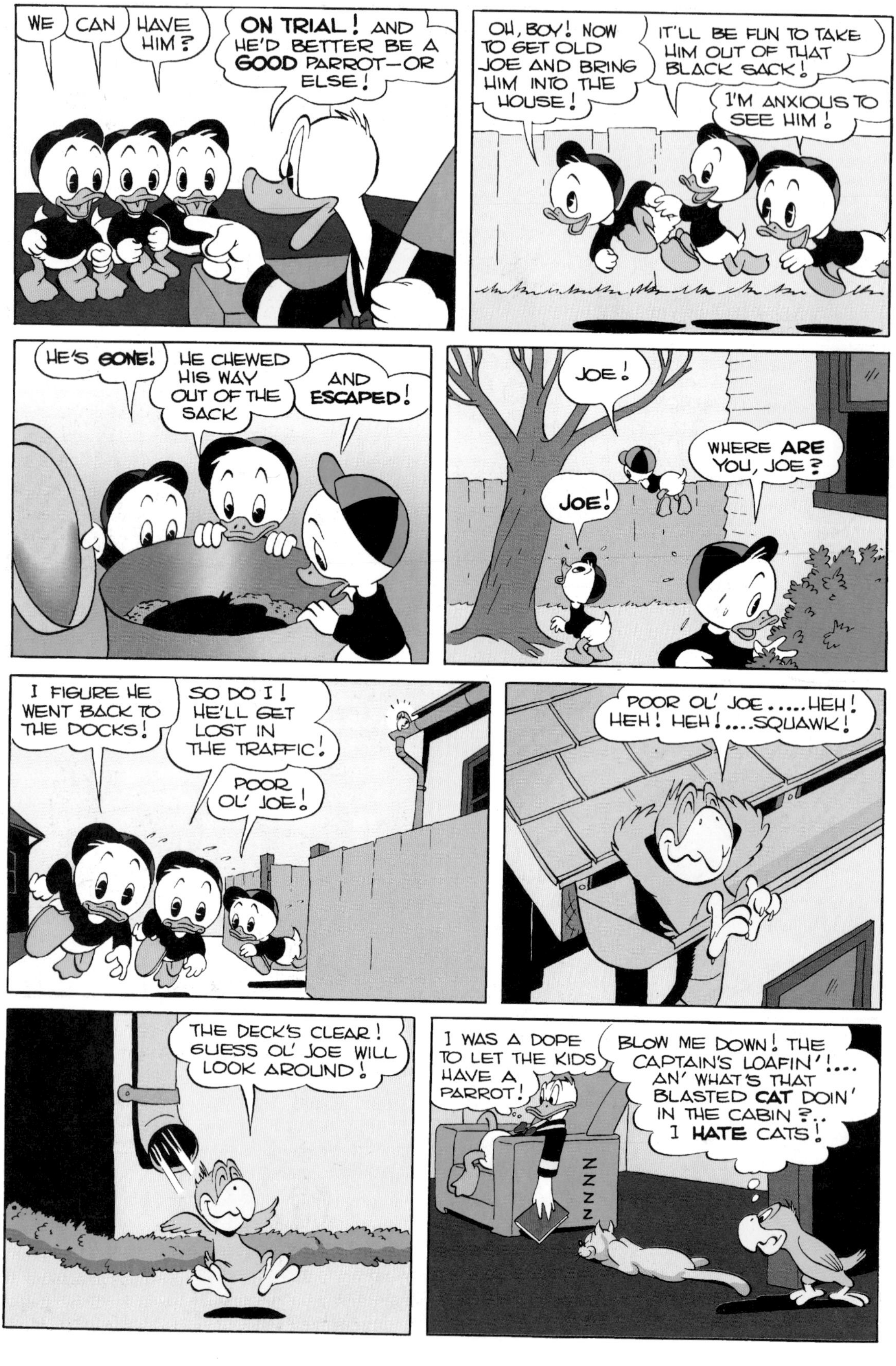
WE
CAN
HAVE HIM?
ON TRIAL! AND HE'D BETTER BE A GOOD PARROT—OR ELSE!
OH, BOY! NOW TO GET OLD JOE AND BRING HIM INTO THE HOUSE!
IT'LL BE FUN TO TAKE HIM OUT OF THAT BLACK SACK!
I'M ANXIOUS TO SEE HIM!
HE'S GONE!
HE CHEWED HIS WAY OUT OF THE SACK
AND ESCAPED!
JOE!
WHERE ARE YOU, JOE?
JOE!
I FIGURE HE WENT BACK TO THE DOCKS!
SO DO I! HE'LL GET LOST IN THE TRAFFIC!
POOR OL' JOE!
POOR OL' JOE.....HEH! HEH! HEH!....SQUAWK!
THE DECK'S CLEAR! GUESS OL' JOE WILL LOOK AROUND!
I WAS A DOPE TO LET THE KIDS HAVE A PARROT!
BLOW ME DOWN! THE CAPTAIN'S LOAFIN'!... AN' WHAT'S THAT BLASTED CAT DOIN' IN THE CABIN?.. I HATE CATS!
ZZZZ

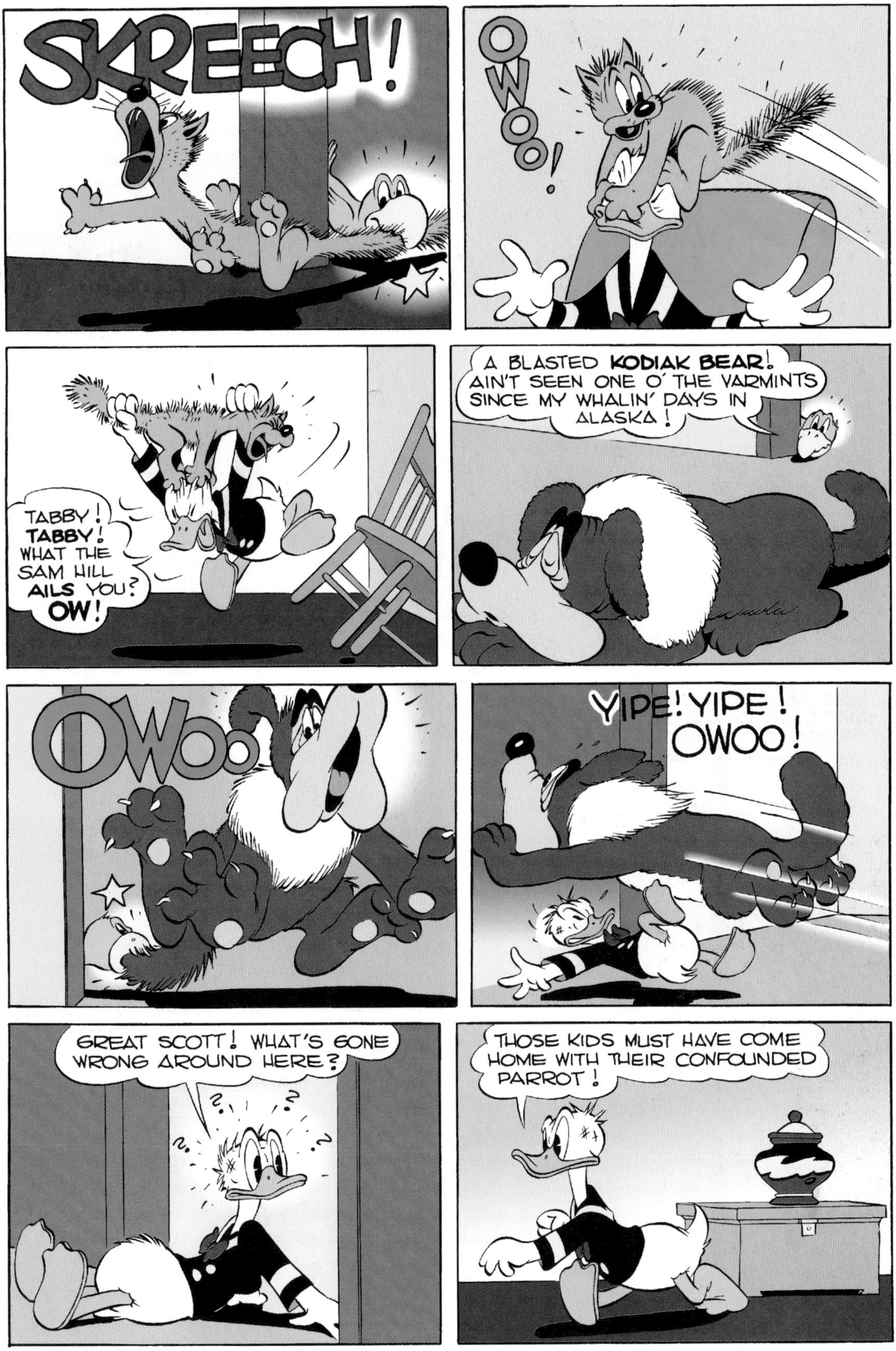
SKREECH!
OWOO!
TABBY! TABBY! WHAT THE SAM HILL AILS YOU? OW!
A BLASTED KODIAK BEAR! AIN'T SEEN ONE O' THE VARMINTS SINCE MY WHALIN' DAYS IN ALASKA!
OWOO
YIPE! YIPE! OWOO!
GREAT SCOTT! WHAT'S GONE WRONG AROUND HERE?
THOSE KIDS MUST HAVE COME HOME WITH THEIR CONFOUNDED PARROT!

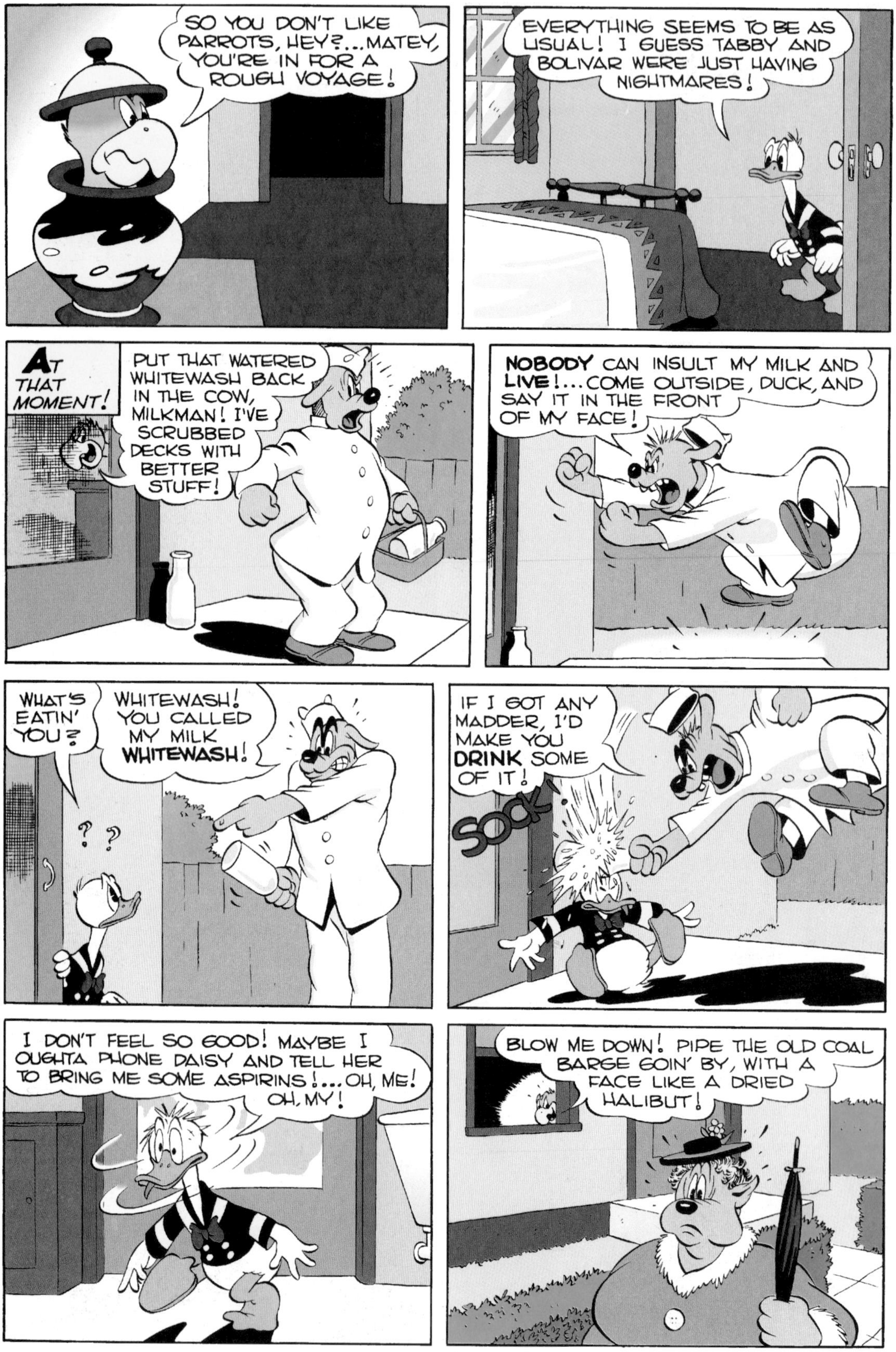
SO YOU DON'T LIKE PARROTS, HEY?... MATEY, YOU'RE IN FOR A ROUGH VOYAGE!
EVERYTHING SEEMS TO BE AS USUAL! I GUESS TABBY AND BOLIVAR WERE JUST HAVING NIGHTMARES!
AT THAT MOMENT!
PUT THAT WATERED WHITEWASH BACK IN THE COW, MILKMAN! I'VE SCRUBBED DECKS WITH BETTER STUFF!
NOBODY CAN INSULT MY MILK AND LIVE!... COME OUTSIDE, DUCK, AND SAY IT IN THE FRONT OF MY FACE!
WHAT'S EATIN' YOU?
WHITEWASH! YOU CALLED MY MILK WHITEWASH!
IF I GOT ANY MADDER, I'D MAKE YOU DRINK SOME OF IT!
SOCK!
I DON'T FEEL SO GOOD! MAYBE I OUGHTA PHONE DAISY AND TELL HER TO BRING ME SOME ASPIRINS!... OH, ME! OH, MY!
BLOW ME DOWN! PIPE THE OLD COAL BARGE GOIN' BY, WITH A FACE LIKE A DRIED HALIBUT!

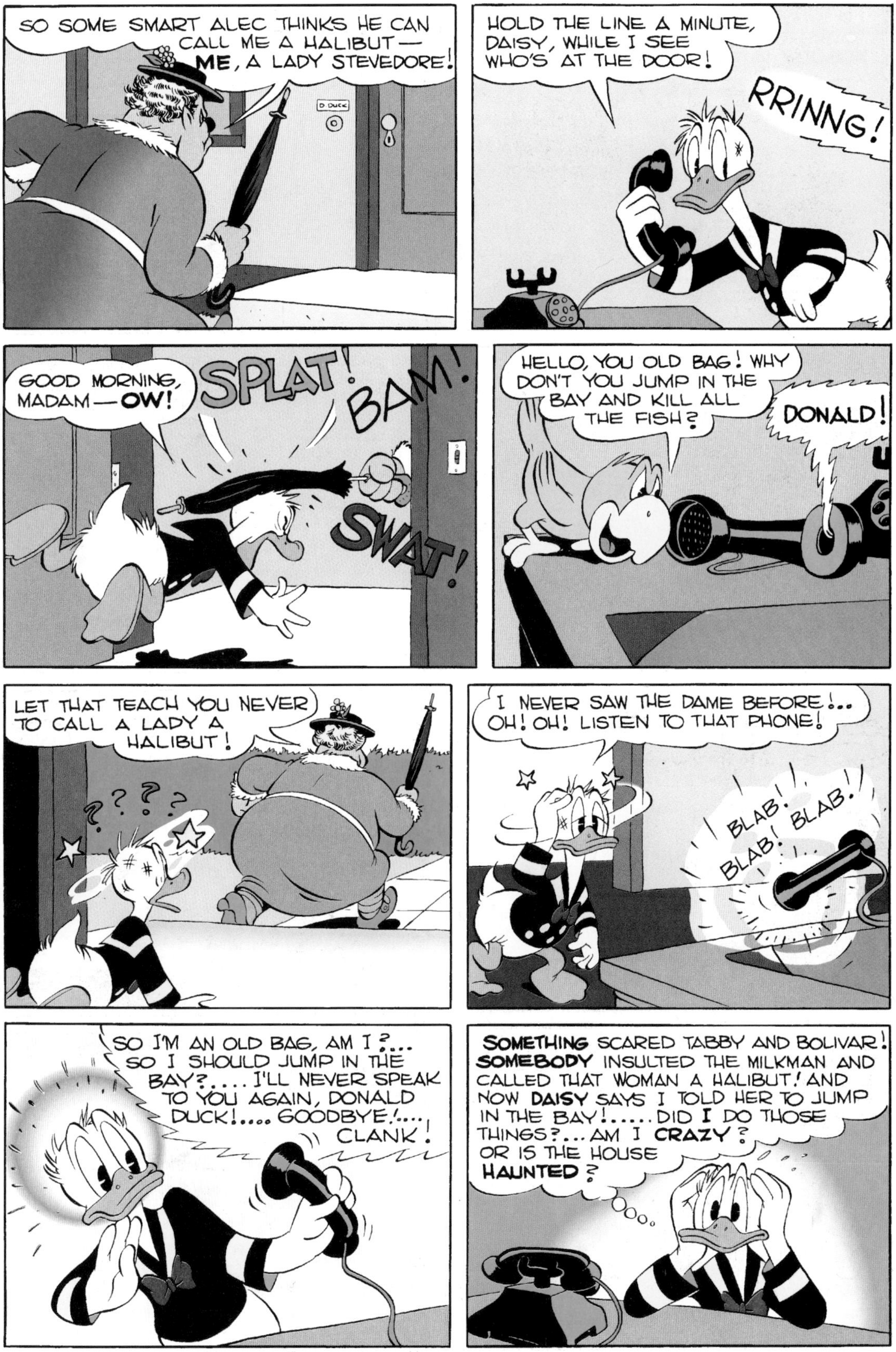
SO SOME SMART ALEC THINKS HE CAN CALL ME A HALIBUT— ME, A LADY STEVEDORE!
D DUCK
HOLD THE LINE A MINUTE, DAISY, WHILE I SEE WHO'S AT THE DOOR!
RRINNG!
GOOD MORNING, MADAM—OW!
SPLAT!
BAM!
SWAT!
HELLO, YOU OLD BAG! WHY DON'T YOU JUMP IN THE BAY AND KILL ALL THE FISH?
DONALD!
LET THAT TEACH YOU NEVER TO CALL A LADY A HALIBUT!
I NEVER SAW THE DAME BEFORE!.. OH! OH! LISTEN TO THAT PHONE!
BLAB! BLAB! BLAB!
SO I'M AN OLD BAG, AM I?... SO I SHOULD JUMP IN THE BAY?.... I'LL NEVER SPEAK TO YOU AGAIN, DONALD DUCK!.... GOODBYE!....
CLANK!
SOMETHING SCARED TABBY AND BOLIVAR! SOMEBODY INSULTED THE MILKMAN AND CALLED THAT WOMAN A HALIBUT! AND NOW DAISY SAYS I TOLD HER TO JUMP IN THE BAY!..... DID I DO THOSE THINGS?... AM I CRAZY? OR IS THE HOUSE HAUNTED?

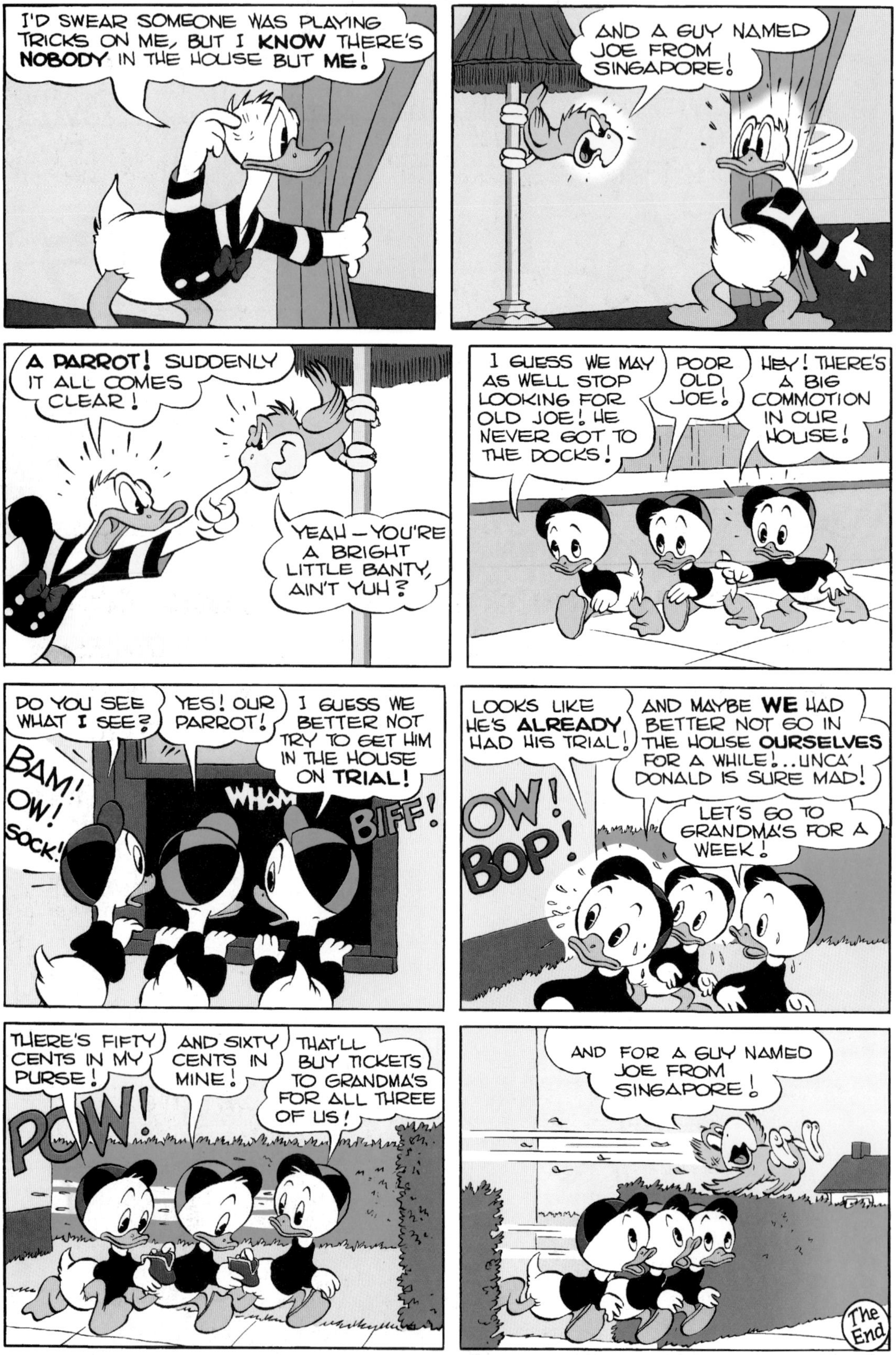
I'D SWEAR SOMEONE WAS PLAYING TRICKS ON ME, BUT I KNOW THERE'S NOBODY IN THE HOUSE BUT ME!
AND A GUY NAMED JOE FROM SINGAPORE!
A PARROT! SUDDENLY IT ALL COMES CLEAR!
YEAH—YOU'RE A BRIGHT LITTLE BANTY, AIN'T YUH?
I GUESS WE MAY AS WELL STOP LOOKING FOR OLD JOE! HE NEVER GOT TO THE DOCKS!
POOR OLD JOE!
HEY! THERE'S A BIG COMMOTION IN OUR HOUSE!
DO YOU SEE WHAT I SEE?
YES! OUR PARROT!
I GUESS WE BETTER NOT TRY TO GET HIM IN THE HOUSE ON TRIAL!
BAM! OW! SOCK!
WHAM
BIFF!
LOOKS LIKE HE'S ALREADY HAD HIS TRIAL!
AND MAYBE WE HAD BETTER NOT GO IN THE HOUSE OURSELVES FOR A WHILE!..UNCA' DONALD IS SURE MAD!
OW! BOP!
LET'S GO TO GRANDMA'S FOR A WEEK!
THERE'S FIFTY CENTS IN MY PURSE!
AND SIXTY CENTS IN MINE!
THAT'LL BUY TICKETS TO GRANDMA'S FOR ALL THREE OF US!
POW!
AND FOR A GUY NAMED JOE FROM SINGAPORE!
The End

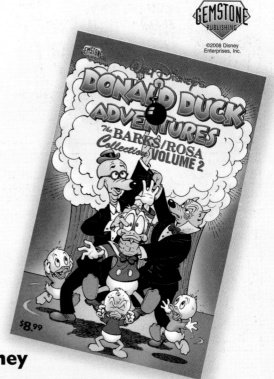

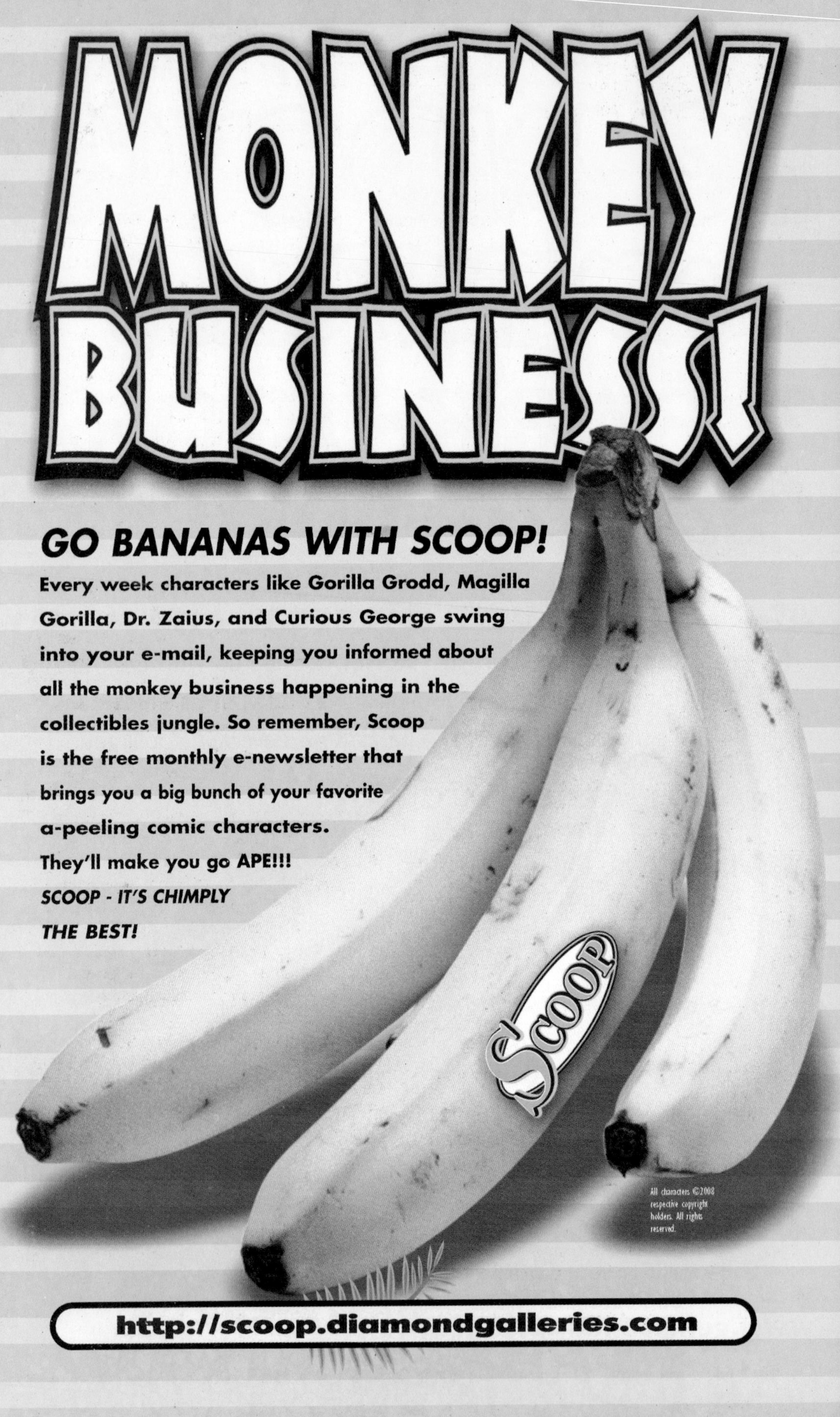
MONKEY BUSINESS!
GO BANANAS WITH SCOOP!
Every week characters like Gorilla Grodd, Magilla Gorilla, Dr. Zaius, and Curious George swing into your e-mail, keeping you informed about all the monkey business happening in the collectibles jungle. So remember, Scoop is the free monthly e-newsletter that brings you a big bunch of your favorite a-peeling comic characters.
They'll make you go APE!!!
SCOOP - IT'S CHIMPLY THE BEST!
Scoop
All characters ©2008 respective copyright holders. All rights reserved.
http://scoop.diamondgalleries.com